About the Author

Paddy finally forgave Emma for her past and they went on to marry and have seven children, Amy, Rose, Diesel, Ice, Lolly, Pistol and Ball. Emma allowed Paddy to choose the names as a way of an apology for her chequered past. Amy went on to become the bestest doctor in the world, because she is magical, like her father. Cunt was eventually kicked out of Paddy's head. He jumped the train to London and climbed into the head of Boris Johnson, where he still lives to this day, influencing all of Boris's major decisions.

The Confessions of a Captain's Addiction

Paddy

The Confessions of a Captain's Addiction

Olympia Publishers
London

www.olympiapublishers.com
OLYMPIA PAPERBACK EDITION

A CIP catalogue record for this title is
available from the British Library.

ISBN: 978-1-80074-569-8

This book is memoir. It reflects the author's present recollections of
experiences over time. Some names and characteristics have been
changed, some events have been compressed, and some dialogue
has been recreated. The opinions expressed in this book are the
author's own and do not reflect the views of the publisher, author's
employer, organisation, committee or other group or individual.

First Published in 2023

Olympia Publishers
Tallis House
2 Tallis Street
London
EC4Y 0AB

Printed in Great Britain

Dedication

I would like to dedicate this book to my beautiful daughter
Amy. My reason for living.

Introduction

Hello, readers. My name is Paddy. That's my real name. There are no bullshit, made-up fantasies in this book. This is the truth, the grit, the crazy. My life.

As I am writing this book, I am sitting comfortably on a large subsea research vessel in the very respectable rank of First Officer/SDPO (Senior Dynamic Positioning Officer), second in command of a vessel and crew of sixty plus. It sounds like a position of responsibility to most, and indeed it is. It's a disciplined, sometimes stressful, but ultimately rewarding job.

However, please don't be fooled into thinking that this job role and subsequent title will make you believe that I, Paddy the Fuck Up, Paddy the Tit, Paddy the Fucking Baddy is always in this responsible officer headspace. For I am, as you will read throughout this book, a totally unbalanced and totally reckless motherfucker with a history of nearly three decades at sea, twenty-three plus years in rank and five different prisons, with relentless crimes behind me.

I want to document this, hence the book, so that the people closest to my heart, especially my beautiful daughter, Amy, can get some clarity and understanding of what went wrong so many times on this journey of my life so far.

CHAPTER 1
The beast is born

Right. How did I adapt into a professional knob? Well, let's look briefly at my childhood and teenage years. I came from a loving family – mother, father and an elder sister, then in later years, two younger brothers. We never had much in the way of luxuries or material shit; that you find later in life means absolutely fuck all anyway. Not many people in my area did have much in those days, growing up in the eighties. What we did have though was love and respect for one's elders and all the other qualities that are few and far between amongst the natural knobs hitting puberty these days. Now, please bear in mind, I morphed into a knob, became a knob, whereas these little pricks these days have to reverse their direction from already being a knob to being something other than.

That's enough about knobs anyway. What I am getting at is, as you will read you will no doubt say to yourself over and over again, what the fuck did you do that for, you dickhead? Those things are meant to be done by people who came from broken homes and the like (as the books say). Not me. I re-wrote that fucking book and made it my own. No excuses.

My introduction to drugs began when I was around twelve years old. It was a civilised drug. Lager, acceptable in the eyes of our society and seen as harmless by most. Although, in the wrong hands it is just as harmful as heroin and ruins so many lives and kills so many people. Some good, some bad, but it's not to be underestimated.

Palma Nova, Majorca. The first sip. I was twelve years of age. My parents had re-mortgaged our home. We got a few grand in the purse and then boom, we were all flying high. I got a new leather jacket, a pair of Pacino jeans with the patches all over them and a new bike. Although, the bike looked fucking daft, because it had a carrying frame on the back and, annoyingly, one on the front too. So, I looked like fucking Granville from *Open All Hours*, bombing around the streets with a plastic cup jammed in the rear wheel so that I sounded like a motorbike.

Anyway, we were off on our first holiday. A proper holiday, I mean. Majorca, Spain, in a real aeroplane. Off the subject a little bit here. I had a time as a younger child where I would lay in bed, listening to the planes overhead. Wishing that I was up there, going away on holiday. The noise of the jet just sounded calm and serene to me. And now, when it's quiet and I hear a plane overhead, I feel relaxed. I go back, mentally, to that bedroom, as a child. I am not trying to bore the arse out of you here. I just wanted to share that, because it's something that has calmed and equally upset me in so many situations. Laying there as a child, listening to it, and then later down the line, on the top bunk of a bed, in a cell on G wing. But still, back to that same thought process.

Right, that's enough of that shite. So off we go into the sun. Bermuda shorts, flip flops, the whole fucking shebang. I loved it. I had never felt so relaxed in my parents' company. They were different people on holiday. Chilled out. They even bought along my sister's mate, Janet. Gave me something to perv on, try and get a cheeky little peek of a white one popping out of the bra every now and then.

It was there that I spent my twelfth birthday. My dad let me have a bottle of beer. Fuck me it felt good. That feeling of tipsiness and the combination of being relaxed and looking dapper in my new Bermuda shorts and all-over pink lobster tan. I felt on top of the world. I was out on the balcony of our middle-storey apartment howling at the moon, I mean literally. Every car that passed I would shout 'BEEP BEEP'.

I was of course being a total dickhead, but I didn't care. I was making my parents laugh for the first time. I somehow felt like Johnny Hard Arms, Pablo motherfuckin Escobar, untouchable and funny and witty. Just the kind of guy everybody wanted to be. Yeah, I fucking like this, I said to myself. Let's have a sneaky peek in the old Bermuda netting and see how many pubes have blossomed since my last bottle of beer. None, as it happened, but it was a road I was gonna explore. Pissed Paddy was the one. Popeye has his tin of spinach. I had my tin of San Miguel.

That, apart from my dad making us walk about ten miles one day with my mum heavily pregnant with my younger brother, Paul, because he was too tight to pay for a fucking bus, is the only thing I really remember from that holiday. It would have been three if my sister's mate Janet had whipped a tit out.

CHAPTER 2
Meeting the Snail

Okay, so now were back in Blighty. Home again. The purse was diminishing and things were starting to come back down to earth. Skint. I didn't care though. As I mentioned earlier, we never had much anyway, so it wasn't missed. As long as I could get my hands on a bevvy with my mates, I was happy. Four cans of Chieftain Lager were my usual. It had a picture of a massive Apache Indian on the front of the tin. That will be me after a few swigs. Hard as fuck. We would have to get an adult to go into the shop and buy them for us.

The routine was to ask a lad who looked sound. 'Eh, mate, any chance you can go in the shop for us and get us eight cans of Chieftain Lager? Take one for yourself too, mate.' Nine times out of ten it would work, and we would get the butterflies in our bellies and then leg it to the nearest alleyway with our bounty and get tucked in between the bin bags and dog shit and get pissed.

Then, on the other side of that coin, or the one out of them ten, it didn't go to plan, and the lad we deemed sound would say, 'Yeah, no worries, give us the money.' Then he would just walk away with our beer tokens. 'Tell ye what, if I'd of had a tinny before he took our money, I would have battered that twat,' I'd say to my mate. In reality I wouldn't have. I was barely a teenager and had the physique of an X-ray; I couldn't fight sleep.

That would be our night ruined. We would still end in the alleyway amongst the bin bags and dog turds. But instead of getting pissed, we would find a couple of ice lolly sticks and rub them on the concrete to fashion a point, a knife, a shiv, if you're a criminal. And we would then go searching for ants and stab the shit out of them, taking our frustrations out on the poor ants. I reckon that in the seventies, ants would walk from A to B in a straight line. Then in the eighties, frustrated little cunts like me and my mates made the entire ant population break formation and zig zag all over the place, legging it around like a sniper's nightmare.

Then, on one of our successful nights, we were introduced to a lad called Dave Snail. I actually thought that was his real name, but it wasn't. He actually looked like a fucking snail. He looked like his face had been on fire and put out with a spade, proper flat face with tentacles. No kidding: no tentacles but an odd resemblance to a snail. A walking buffet if the cunt ever went to France. Anyway, Snaily, as he became known to us, was a seasoned pothead and I must say a very talented musician. He was right into Pink Floyd. Which got me into them. Love them. His parents were always fucking mashed, off their tits noon and night. So, his house was a place we could go and get fucked up in without any hassle. The new alleyway, if you like.

That's when I had my first joint. Fuck fucking me. Suddenly I started to take notice of shit I'd never noticed before. 'Look, lads, them fucking stars up there – proper fucking shiny, aren't they, eh? I wonder if there're any little star men living on them, or starfish. Do you reckon starfish are aliens? Is there a sea on those stars for fish to live in? They might have run out of water and all the starfish fell onto our planet.,' Weed man. It's killing my Popeye image, this. I don't feel hard any more. I feel a little bit paranoid but giggly. I don't really care to be honest. I'm fucking stoned.

This went on for a few years. They (whoever the fuck they are) say that one drug leads to another. It does and it doesn't. It did in my case. However, the dynamics of the individual, i.e., what that person wants from the experience, determines if there will be a next level, in reality. That's what I believe anyway. And I have had, at times, more drugs in my system than a pharmacy has on its shelves.

We sort of fell out of contact with Snaily. I can't remember why. I think we were all growing as individuals, as you do. Getting a bit more of a zest for life, and he was essentially holding us back. I think that was the reason anyway. I do remember bumping into him when I was eighteen years of age. Fucking Highlander. I knew everything. Anyway, I remember he was in front of me, in a street. Same street where he lived, funnily enough. He didn't travel to far from his den, did ol' Snaily. There was this guy in front of me, just squatting sporadically, shouting, 'DOOFA, DOOFA.'

I thought, right. There are two options here that determine the man in front of me. Option one. He is engaged in the art of some new fitness technique. Option two. He is just batshit fucking crazy. When I got parallel with this fitness fanatic nutcase, it was Snaily. 'Fuckinell, Dave, I didn't recognise you without your shell.' Kidding, I didn't say that. I said something along the lines of, 'Fuck me, Dave, hello mate, it's me. Paddy.' He just stared at me, on the third ring of Saturn behind the eyes. Then, out of the blue, 'DOOFA.' The cunt goes down again.

It was then I realised what he was doing. He was picking up cigarette stumps from the floor, and the DOOFA was his shortened version of, *do for later*, DOOFA. 'Okay, mate, see ye later,' I said, and off I went. I never have seen or heard of him since. He is probably sitting off on a lettuce somewhere, throwing stones at the moon. If you're reading this, Dave, I apologise for the insults. But fuck me, mate, you do look like a snail.

CHAPTER 3
School's out

My dad decided to remove me from school at the age of fifteen. Pre-GCSEs. Not a wise move, most would say, but after years of constant conflict and shit from the school, plus bad reports, suspensions, etc. (when I could be bothered to attend school), he realised that I wasn't to be an academic. So he decided that the only other option was manual labour, which to be fair I preferred.

I remember getting ready for school one morning. My dad had been out on the ale the night before, and as per usual he came home, ate his dinner, went to the bathroom for a piss, and then, as I imagine, he just walked out of his clothes as he left the bathroom. I would stay awake until I heard him going to bed, and then I would let out a large yawn (trying to sound casual as I headed to the bathroom for a piss). I was, in fact, going on a raid. My dad always had shitloads of loose change in his pockets, and I needed cash for my ciggies.

Going to school with no cigarettes was to me a bit like going into a brothel for a hug. Fucking pointless. I would never learn my three times tables without a smoke break. Anyway. So off I went into the bathroom. My dad's trousers were laying on the floor, next to a pair of underpants, just lying there looking all aggressive, sunny side up. Right, let's get into them pockets. The underpants growl at me as I get closer. Into the pocket. Ohhhhh, look. There're a few fifty pence pieces there. Ohhhh, and a few twenties too. Weird, that: a 20p piece is a bit like a 50p piece but smaller. A bit like a baby 50p.

'Paddy, you're fucking stoned again. Stop admiring the fucking coins, get the job done and get the fuck out of here before somebody comes in and catches you. Or worst case scenario, his underpants come to life and leap onto your face like that fucking thing of the movie, *Aliens*, and for fuck's sake, don't let the prize jangle as you pass their bedroom. Yawn again – that sounds normal.'

Yep, so it was the next morning after that particular raid. I had gotten dressed for school, a coin in each pocket, separated so they didn't rattle. (Already learning the criminal ways.) I walked past my parents' bedroom, and I heard that noise that I always dreaded. 'Patrick.' I usually only got called that name when I had done something wrong, amongst other things.

'Oh shit,' I thought. 'I've been nicked. Run, Paddy, escape.'

'Patrick,' my dad shouted again. I pushed open his bedroom door. My dad was just lying on the bed, in a pose, what looked like the Kate Winslett scene from *Titanic*, where she is being painted, the blanket covering his love spuds. 'I am taking you out of that school. It's not doing you any good. So go and take off that uniform. You are not going back to that place.'

'Am I grounded?' I said.

'No, son, you're just not going back,' he said.

Happy fucking days. Obviously, I didn't say that, otherwise I would have been volleyed all over the house. All I could think to say was, 'Well, can I still play out?'

'Of course you can, son.'

So, for a good few months I was just cutting around the streets, alone during the days, whilst my mates were all in school. There were four of us at the start, including myself. Close mates. Nothing like the Goonies. We didn't have bikes for a start. Anyway, we were around fourteen to sixteen years of age.

The four of us, hanging around together. Tommo, he was a couple of years older than the rest of us. He was always spotless: he loved himself, with his perfect middle part in his hair. Then there was Joey, who unfortunately went in the wrong direction and became a full-on heroin and crack addict, then later in life an alcoholic. Just basically swapping one addiction for another. He was, and still is, a good lad with a good, pure heart, but he got that life sentence that heroin brings with it.

Not many people recover from heroin addiction. The ones that do kick the habit usually, as they see it, downgrade to alcohol to maintain that state, a sort of high. Although, as I've already mentioned earlier, it's not a fucking downgrade, not at all. It's just as addictive, albeit over a different timescale, as heroin. I visited Joey a few weeks back in the care home he now lives in. His appearance has been totally savaged by drugs and drink alike. Never to return to what society would deem as normal, in both appearance and the way he moves and talks.

Then there was Peter. An odd-looking lad from a very weird family. His father was very Joseph Fritzl. I am sure he was having relations with his daughters. It's a bit bad of me to say that, I agree, but they were all very hillbillyish, that type of thing. All very talented on the banjo too, funnily enough. One of Peter's two talents was to pick locks. The other was to repel girls. Smelly bastard, he was. He would pick the lock on the back of his TV at home and get the 50p pieces out of it. He always had money, did Peter. I actually, as a grown adult, held Peter up at gunpoint at his workplace. That's coming later in the show.

Tommo, who was a keen angler, met this older guy, sort of dad age, called Steve. He met him whilst fishing. We would go to Steve's house in the evenings to smoke weed. Now, Steve didn't smoke weed or in fact drink alcohol. He would just drink bucketloads of tea and smoked cigarettes that were about twelve feet long, one after the other. Although he was only about four feet in height, so the ciggies were probably just normal sized, they just sort of looked huge against his tiny frame and pinhead.

Anyway, around the era, sort of middle of the Steve days, Peter, the fucking oddball, went his own separate way. So it was left with just the trio, myself, Joey and Tommo. We were always stoned. Looking back, it was a good time. For them few months I wasn't hurting anybody. I was just marching to the beat of my own drums. Getting stoned out of my head, then going home to bed and repeating the process the following day. Steve, a good guy all around to be fair, was funding our habit. I think deep down he was just glad of the company in the evenings.

I remember this one night. I got absolutely fucking wasted, stoned, on a different level. I got home from Steve's at around eleven p.m. Now usually my parents were tucked up in bed at this point, asleep. They would usually leave a lamp on downstairs for me coming home. So I put the key in the lock. I was thinking, 'Aren't locks amazing, eh, the way the locks just know the keys. I mean, there must be millions if not billions of keys and if you try them, the lock will just go, nope, until it gets the right key.'

Paddy. It's a fucking key, you prick, you're stoned. Just open the fucking door, I said to myself. So, the door opens. Hang on, I can hear noises. It's the TV, somebody's up, shit. Okay, Paddy, relax, I thought. It's probably just my sister and her mate, Janet. Oh, I might see a tit. Yeah, man, head up, shoulders back, pigeon chest out. So, I entered into the living room, eyes like a Chinaman. And who is there? My parents. Watching the TV. Shit, I thought. I am way too fucking stoned to deal with this.

Now I have a bit of a dilemma here. If I say goodnight and escape upstairs to my bedroom, they will surely know that I am up to something because I never do that. So, I will have to do something normal, something they would expect me to do. So, with that I goes into the kitchen. I get a bowl out, the cornflakes, the milk, the sugar and the spoon. I then go back into the living room with my bowl. I then park my arse on the sofa next to my dad's feet.

It always annoyed the shit out of me, the way my dad would be sprawled out on the sofa like fucking Spartacus. I would come for a sit down and he would move his feet about six inches. I could barely get my bony arse in the gap. A bit like sitting next to a big fat fucker on a small aircraft. I'm not calling my dad a big fat fucker; that's way too tame for me. I was just referencing the space.

Anyway. This is all normal, Paddy, I thought. Just watch the fucking TV and eat your cornflakes; it's all good, Paddy, honest. But I could feel and see my dad staring at me through my peripheral vision. A quick glance to the left at my mum: fuck me, she's staring at me too. What's wrong with these people? Eyes to the floor, Paddy lad. Oh fuck me, even Sheba the dog's looking at me oddly, her head tilted to one side with those confused eyes.

'What's wrong?' I said.

'What the fuck have you been taking, son?' my dad said.

'Nothing,' I said, a bit too high-pitched, as if I was about to burst into a song.

'You have been taking something,' my mum said. Oh fuck me, I thought, I am being fucking tag-team here. If Sheba the dog asks me the same question, I am fucking bolting out of the door. Thank God Sheba remained silent, but when I looked further down I realised what the accusations were all about. Paddy, you dozy bastard, I thought, you have forgotten the fucking cornflakes. I had been sitting there, off my fucking trolley, drinking milk like a fucking cat out of a bowl. You dickhead, I thought.

'Erm, I'm going to bed,' I said.

'I think you better had, son.' BEEP BEEP. Off I went like the fuckin road runner up the stairs.

Another time I remember me trying to act normal. I made my mum a cup of coffee, stoned off my bastard head again. I must have been in the kitchen for ages, because my mum came in to check what was taking me so long. 'Patrick, what's taking you so long' she said.

I was standing over the cup with the coffee in, just staring at the cup, and then I looked at her like she was stupid and said, 'I'm waiting for it to stop steaming, aren't I.' Fuck me, is she stupid? I can't carry that, the fucking steam will go everywhere. What a fucking response, looking back. Honestly, that's the level of stonedness I was reaching. Crossing traffic lights would confuse the shite out of me. I would stand there, waiting to cross, just fucking zombied, waiting on a green light and then step out in front of cars when the lights changed. Shit, the green's for the cars, Paddy, you dickhead, not you. The green man is for you. Or is it the red man? Fuck, I can't remember. Here we go again. Why can't they just say go? Or don't go? So confusing.

I suppose that most people, or teens as I was at that time, would have said to themselves, fuck this, this is getting me nowhere, this. It's gonna get me killed. But not me. I fucking loved it. I think it was the departure from being me that was what I liked. I never did like myself much back then. I mean me. I found myself a bit boring and needy and a bit of a wanker to be honest. But when I was fucked up I didn't care about anything really. I certainly didn't have those nagging doubts about myself, jabbing constantly at me. I never had confidence in any way back then. When I was sober, I hated that. Stoned, I didn't care what I thought. As I say, crossing the road was challenging enough. I do like myself now though. Love myself in fact. I can't keep out of the mirror.

CHAPTER 4
YTS

YTS. It stands for Youth Training Scheme, a scheme offered, in my teens, to the youth. Hence the name. It offered a set wage of £29.50 per week plus travel expenses to the under seventeens and a massive £35.00 plus expenses to the over seventeens.

Mine started at a place called Gostin Craft Workshop. It was a carpentry outfit, making cabinets and the like. It was all proper handcrafted gear too, dovetail joints and mortice and tenon joints. Just the word 'joint' made me want to sign up. It was my dad's idea. My dad's dream, not mine. His vision of me becoming fucking Zeberdee (I think that's his name. Pinocchio's dad. Master carpenter) and starting a business building bespoke furniture.

I sort of came round to the idea. I was good with wood and glue and shit. I had made an arsenal of weapons in the past out of ice lolly sticks. Glue – well, I will leave that to your imagination. I actually was sacked from this job because of glue. That combined with taking a piss in the canteen kettle and spiking one of the supervisors with magic mushrooms. This brought the board of directors to the conclusion that I wasn't fit for Gostin Craft Workshop. Unfair dismissal, I would argue.

There were, I would say from memory, around twenty plus sixteen-year-olds on this course that started together. We were give our own workbench and introduced to our tools kits. Proper carpentry tools they were. Learn the basics before moving on to machinery was their sort of motto. I like this, I thought. I have

24

my own table, tools. Give me some wood and glue and nails and shit and let's get these fucking units built. I love this. Well, fuck me. In comes the supervisors with the, how to work out angles for this, and tenth of a sixteenth cutting curves and blah, blah, fucking blah. I hate this. Why is it so hard? It's worse than school. I want to go home. Why do I need to know maths to make a fucking shelf?

So after a couple of months of trying to work out the angle of the dangle type of thing, I just gave up. It wasn't registering. I didn't want it basically. I reverted to the true me. I would smoke a joint at lunchtime then eat a pasty and a strawberry tart from the bakers, fill my pockets with sweets, mojos and jellies to curb the munchies and the boredom, and then back to fucking about, acting the clown. It was during one of these acting performances I was pinged on CCTV and subsequently sacked for chucking wood glue at a lad called Jamie. I just thought it would be funny to get white wood glue in his long, curly black hair. And yes, CCTV. It was a thing even back then. I honestly believe it was installed because of me. Especially in the canteen above the kettle.

If you are reading this, Mr Gostin, thank you for sacking me. It wasn't really for me anyway. Not my cup of tea, pardon the pun. I did learn one thing from your workshop though. As Confucius the philosopher would say, 'The wise man should never stick his cock in a full kettle that has just been boiled.'

CHAPTER 5
Toe to toe with Tommo

My mate, Tommo. Perfect middle parting and a set of gnashers that Mr Colgate himself would kill for. He incidentally had a job involving wood and glue and staples and shit. It was making frames for settees and chairs. It was only about half a mile from Gostin's. His wasn't YTS. It was proper employment. I can't for the life of me recall the name of this place. What I do remember is that it was owned by a pair of old brothers. Proper old miserable bastards, and their wives, the accountants. Probably swingers too. They had that oddity about them, the creepy bastard look. Their operations offices were upstairs in the factory. It just stunk of stale piss and death. It was like God's waiting room up there. I had the misfortune of sitting in that office for an interview. One of the brothers had one eye bigger than the other and was madder than a tree full of fish. Crazy what you remember, isn't it?

'Anyhow, Patrick. How would you feel if I were to say to you that you can start work here on Monday?'

What I wanted to say was, 'I would feel exactly the same as I do now, but I would know I was starting work on Monday.' However, for the sake of good order I gave it the old, 'Oh nice one, thank you so much. I promise I will work really really hard. Can I put my clothes back on now please?' I had got another job, and I was working with Tommo too.

Tommo, however, since starting at this place a few months earlier, had become a bit to close and pally with another lad who worked there, the bastard. He was splitting up the trio. What had happened was, this other lad, the intruder, the Tommo robber, he had a sister, who fell for Tommo's teeth and perfect middle parting. They actually went on to marry and have two beautiful kids, so fair play. However, at the time this was treason. Tommo was leaving me and Joey.

So I worked there for a month or so, giving the outsider the evil stay-away-from-my-Tommo looks. Then for some reason, headache, earache, ball ache. I can't really remember, but something was aching one day. So after refusing an examination from one of the brother's wives, I was sent home to rest. The journey home was an hour or so by bus.

As I was walking out of the factory, I spotted Tommo's cassette recorder, (the original MP3, kids) by his locker. To this day I swear I was borrowing it for the journey home, which sort of rules out the earache I mentioned before. Anyway, Tommo saw me take it and assumed I was stealing it. To this day I believe he just wanted a reason to split up the group. So he comes after me shouting. Net result, we ended up slugging it out in the car park. It was swiftly broken up. Tommo immediately whipped out a comb and straightened his hair. I however, as the newbie and suspected thief, was sacked. Again. FFS.

CHAPTER 6
Take three

This, Paddy boy, isn't looking too fucking rosy, is it? I said to myself. Sixteen years of age and already sacked from two jobs for what I know now to be gross misconduct, but back then in my head I truly believed it was because my employers were pricks with no sense of humour. What's wrong with these people?

I made up some fabricated piss-poor lie to lie to my parents. I can't remember exactly what I said, but I was essentially passing the blame for my dismissal to the dissmissee. (I know that last word is not in the dictionary, but it's my fucking book, so it is now.) They didn't believe me. I was a walking lie. Any person, I don't care who you are, can only deal with any situation, with what that person believes that situation to be, i.e., the long and short being that you need all the information and facts presented to come to a fair conclusion.

Now, due to me being a prolific habitual liar, it sort of negated the above ruling. And the conclusion drawn was, Patrick's lying again. It's only as you get older, more mature, that your brain begins to successfully process and understand consequence analysis, i.e., the consequences of one's actions, combined with the risk factors. Now, you can't really manage a risk unless you understand that risk. And you can't process the severity or consequence when you are as high as a fucking kite twenty-four hours a day, seven days a week. The brain naturally wants the drug more, so it prioritises that and stores it on the top shelf of the thought/rational processing and subsequently shelves the consequence elsewhere, out of sight.

In my case I think my think my brain just opened up my ear-lobe and chucked consequence out. You don't need that, Paddy lad. The latter is through the eyes of somebody with a drug issue. Me. I am not trying to imply that all people's minds operate this way. If they did then we would all be drugged up. And the world would be a happier place. Kidding.

So I am back to square one. Or square zero. Stoned, skint and jobless. I was of course funding my habit through other means, which are documented in my next book *(Paddy. The First Semi.)*. I had heard about another scheme, again YTS, that offered young men the opportunity to start a career at sea. I actually heard about this scheme through Peter the odd ball, whom I still occasionally had contact with. This scheme, Saint Paul's Trust, trained lads for a three-month period on basic seamanship skills and then sent them off to a sponsor shipping company.

Peter had completed the three-month training. He was then then sent off to London to join a cargo vessel at Tilbury docks. However, due to him being a weird little oddity, when he arrived in London, he couldn't find the ship. So instead of simply asking for directions, he just jumped on a train and headed home again. That was his sea career over before it began. He never even made it to the gangway, the fucking idiot.

Me, however, I latched onto this idea and attended a sort of interview with the guy who ran the course, Mike Kuelamens, or the Kooly dude as we all called him. He was a great bloke. He has recently written a book about the trust and the trainees involved; look it up. I am in it, sooo famous is I. He had a true passion for what he was doing. He actually wanted us to succeed, fly the nest if you like. So I passed the interview, and then I goes home to tell my mum.

'Eh, mum, do you remember when I nearly broke my hand as a kid?' I don't think she did. What had happened: ack to Popeye again. Before-the-alcohol Popeye. I can't really remember the exact age I was, but I remember vividly asking my mum to make me spinach, thinking that I would instantly become like the cartoon Popeye. I don't mean all colourful and with a pipe; I mean strong and hard as fuck and without the stupid voice.

It's no wonder Popeye couldn't get the woman, Olive. It had nothing to do with his strength; it was because he sounded like a gobshite and smoked a pipe. His breath must have stunk, and can you imagine what his farts would smell like, chinning tins of spinach like that. Olive looked like a crackhead anyway, way too skinny, with no arse and a flat chest. Betty Boo, Popeye, my old snowflake, she looks, perky should we say, and she was always smiling. Olive was just playing the field, couldn't make her mind up that one.

Anyway, my mum made me this spinach. So immediately after forcing down this awful meal, I went outside and punched a wall, believing the wall would just collapse, like in the cartoon. Obviously it didn't and I nearly broke my bastard hand. Crying my fucking eyes out I was. You need to get onto Ofcom, people. That's false advertising that is. It's a bit like the deodorant, Lynx Africa. It smells fuck all like Africa, people, believe me. I was there for three years.

Anyway, apologies, I went a bit off-piste there. 'Mum, do you remember when I nearly broke my hand as a kid'? She gave me one of those, what the fuck are you talking about sort of looks. 'Well anyway, Mum, I nearly broke my hand because I thought I was Popeye, and now like Popeye I am going to go to sea.'

'What are you taking now, Patrick?' she said.

'Nothing, Mum, I am not taking anything,' I said.

'Well, why are you wearing your sister's dress with the dog's collar around your neck?' Kidding. I was actually in my shell suit. The rich kids had La Coste shell suits with a crocodile badge on them. Mine had a ginger cat on my badge. A sort of Lo Coste tracksuit. It had pot bombs all over it (the hole made when a bit of weed resin falls out of the joint you are smoking onto your clothes). That was the thing about shell suits. If you dropped just a tiny pot bomb on your thigh you would lose half a leg if you didn't catch it quickly.

Off-piste again, aren't I. Sorry. Yep, so I explained my new career intentions to my mum. She just sort of said, 'Okay, Patrick' and walked away.

Then in comes my dad from work later on. 'Dad,' I said, 'I am going to sea.' My poor dad looked like he just wanted to spin around and head back out the door again.

'What?' he said. So again I explained. The response I got from him, I still remember to this day word for word. 'They will use you as a fucking bum bag.' Is it any wonder I didn't have confidence whilst sober? Stoned, I would just think, oh nice one, my dad thinks I am a handsome lad. Sober, I knew what he was referring to, and furthermore I didn't want my dad to speak to me like this and bracket me in this way. I don't hold any of this against my dad. I was a little bastard and he had tried his best with me, or what he believed at that time to be his best. Although like myself, he has become a better version of his true self over the years and has held the family together. Love ye, Dad.

Anyway, so I joined up to this Saint Paul's Trust scheme. It had changed its training method from a three-month YTS route to a nine-month route, both in sea school and additionally at a secondary school. The emphasis being, learn both seamanship skills whilst gaining GCSEs in maths and geography. I excelled in the seamanship but not the GCSEs. I still, at that time, didn't want to, or think I would need maths or school shite in my future career. I was going on a ship, for fuck's sake. Why did I need to know what seventy-four divided by two was? It's like washing your feet with your socks on. Fucking pointless.

It wasn't until later in my sea career that I found out that maths was the key to becoming a navigator, understanding and applying trigonometry and algebra to work out how to get from A to B and estimating positions using stars and sites. Ship's stability. Cross curves for Simpson's rules of naval architecture. Formulas for determining the value of a vessel's centre of gravity and buoyancy. Righting levers, etc. Suddenly, I thought, those supervisors at Gostin Craft Workshop could have furnished me with a stepping stone. Anyhow, I also excelled at this further down the line. Why? Because I wanted it.

My good mate, Thomas, from school, was also on this course. A great lad, Thomas, legend. He joined the same shipping company as me and then went on to have an amazing career with P&O Cruises. After having a litter of kids later on in life, he then hung up his anchor type of thing. He now works on the docks. We had a fucking great time in sea school.

My parents, believing that I had stabilised and was on a true career path, sort of left me alone and just let me get on with it. I was still stoned noon and night and still having to fund my habit somehow. There were two lads on the course with us that didn't sort of fit in. They were posh, well-to-do, with well-off parents. The rest of us were council estate types. Rough and ready and a bit dim. These two didn't slot into that stereotype. Boydee and Ian, they were called. Proper fucking dickheads they were. Or so we though at that time. They were actually nic e and decent lads looking back, but back then, simply because they didn't smoke weed and wanted to study and shit, they were, in our eyes, just a pair of wankers.

They were a little older than us at that time and obviously would be older than us now at this time too. I don't half say some stupid shit, don't I? Crossing them traffic lights again, Paddy, eh. Concentrate. They were older and sensible. Both had cars. Ian's car was an Avenger. Now, this Avenger had an engine problem. It basically made a strange sort of tapping noise when running. Now, me being me, the sneaky, manipulating cunt I was, I saw an opportunity to exploit this and make some cash. I convinced Ian to let me take the car home. I told him that one of my mates was a mechanic and he would happily repair this problem free of charge.

I was only sixteen years old myself. Obviously I didn't have a driving licence. Not a real one anyway. But I knew how to drive; I had owned a couple of cars prior to this (all documented in *Paddy, the First Semi*). So, apprehensively and sort of suspiciously, he handed over the keys. And I mean keys. One for the engine, one for the door and one for the boot. He just wanted to be accepted by the rest of the group after being bullied (not physically) since he had started. I feel a bit bad for that now, but as I've already mentioned, consequence analysis had been chucked out of my lugs. I suppose he thought it was his way in to the group, if you like, his way into the group through me. Hang on, does that mean he was using me? He was playing me, the bastard. I've only just realised that. Ian, you prick. He didn't make it into the group anyway.

So I took this car home and parked it out of sight. I then took it out for manoeuvres that evening. There was myself, Joey and the oddball. We headed to Toxteth, in Liverpool, in the hope of scoring some trips (LSD). We couldn't get our hands on any so we ended up just getting stoned instead. On the way home, I drove through the city centre. I stopped at a set of traffic lights (on the red), 34 not trying to be a smart arse, but I was learning the system. Plus, I normally had a stoned co-pilot next to me for back up.

Next thing, a fucking police van sets off from the lights adjacent to us. Right across the front of our car. Now picture this. I looked around fourteen years of age, skinny and gaunt, fucking dozy-looking. Joey was, and still is, around six foot five, skinhead, and was sporting a huge joint that was hanging from his mouth. He was riding shotgun.

Peter the oddball, who was playing the banjo in the back, practising for the weekly family orgy, I mean, get-together, he just leans forward and fucking points directly at this crossing police van, prompting all eight officers inside to take a closer look at us. 'Fucking hell,' I said. 'That was close. Did you see them all staring at us?' The lights changed and off I went. Next thing, this fucking van just pops up behind us, giving it the old nee-noor-nee-noor-nee-noor blue-light shite.

'Oh shit, I am well and truly fucked here.' Joey, the fucking dickhead, is just hysterical, laughing his head off. Peter, the bell end, just sort of pulled his bottom lip over his head and swallowed. I couldn't see him in the mirror in the backseat, disappeared. This wouldn't be the first time Peter has pulled this trick on me though, as you will find out later. My arse just sort of fell out of me. I fucking curry-bummed it.

Anyway, I pulled over. One of the officers came to my window. 'Turn off the engine and step out of the vehicle, all of you.'

I was trying to act all grown up and of age. 'Okay, sure thing,' I said. Fucking sure thing; why are you speaking like that,

34

I said to myself. You sound like a right knob. So we all exited the vehicle.

'What the fuck is that?' says the officer, pointing to a piece of paper in the window where the tax disc should have been. Ian, the wanker, had cut a perfect circle, taxdisk-shaped, and written the words, 'TAX ON THE WAY'. Ian, I thought, I am going to batter that twat tomorrow. 'Okay,' said the officer. 'What's going on, lads?' I was thinking, I am fucked here. There are eight of them here. They look like they wouldn't have any issues crossing a road in one go, so I am obviously outclassed. Forget about running because I am too stoned. So I just confessed.

'Officer,' I said. 'I am only sixteen. It's not my car. I am sorry.' You know what happened? Jeremy Beadle leapt out with a camera crew and shouted, 'GOTCHA'. No, obviously he didn't. Something better happened. Now this would not, and could not, happen these days.

The officer (my favourite policeman in the whole wide world) gave me back the keys and said to me, like a sheriff to a naughty cowboy, 'You have half an hour to get out of town. I don't want to see you or this vehicle again.' Suddenly, Joey stopped laughing and started looking confused. All I could think of to say was, 'Erm, okay, thanks.' The three officers got back in the car and simply drove off.

'Fucking all right that, wasn't it, boys?' I said, as I started driving around the city centre.

'Where the fuck are you going, Paddy? the plod told us to get out of town,' said Joey.

'Yeah, I know, Joey, but he said we have half an hour.' So I took that thirty minutes and made it my own. Window down, radio cranked up and just fucking cruising. I was legal for half an hour in my head. Any other patrol stops me, and I will tell them, your mate said I was okay for half an hour. I do beg your pardon, sir. So sorry for wasting your time. Off you go, lads. Godspeed.

The next morning, I was up bright and early. 'Good morning, Mum'. My mum just looked at me strangely. What's this little bastard up to? Why is he happy? What does he want? 'I don't want any breakfast, Mum. I am heading into school early.' Such words had never passed my lips before. It just didn't sound natural coming from me. However, truth be told I was happy. I had a fucking massive joint already rolled in my pocket, a car parked around the corner, and I was going to pick my mate Thomas up for sea school.

Unfortunately, I had a bit of a limp. Early hours that morning I had headed to the bathroom for a piss. It was dark and I had kicked my dad's underpants by mistake. I didn't mean to, and furthermore I immediately apologised to them. But they didn't see it this way and attacked my ankle. I couldn't shake them off, so I picked up a bar of soap and threatened them with it. They released their grip and returned to his trousers, growling, brown spit dribbling off them. Nasty bastards, them things, I thought. Should be caged.

That particular day, sea school was at our training vessel, the *Loach*, which was based at Wellington dock, Liverpool. The *Loach* is actually the ship, if you have seen the movie *Buster*, starring Phil Collins. It's about the Great Train Robbery. When he returns from Acapulco, Mexico, you see a ship heading up the River Thames with Phil on it. That's the *Loach*.

Anyway, Thomas and I arrived at the dock, stoned. I parked the car by a café out of sight, and we headed to the vessel. Immediately, fucking Ian's heading towards me. 'Patrick, mate, where's my car?'

'Ian,' I said. 'Don't call me fucking Patrick, call me Crippler, or Cone Finger. That's what all the other girls call me. Listen, you prick, the plod have got your car because you had no fucking tax on it. I am picking it up later on tonight, and I have to pay twenty quid to get it back. I will pay it, and you can pay me back tomorrow.' Lies for profit just flowed naturally from my mouth.

'Okay, thanks,' he said. 'Is it fixed'?

What the fuck is he talking about, fixed, I thought. Oh, the engine. 'Erm, ye, Ian, it's fixed. That's another twenty quid you owe me tomorrow and a tenner for petrol.'

'Okay, I will ask my mum,' he said.

'Oi, fuck off with the asking your mum shit. You're posh. You must have a piggy bank or something. Leave ye mum out of it.'

So that afternoon, lunchtime comes. The weed is wearing off, and my last ten pounds went on petrol and weed last night (thanks, Dad). Fuck it. 'Thomas. Should we take his car to the scrapyard and see if we can weigh it in for some money?' I said.

'Fuck it mate, yeah, let's go for it,' he said. So we loaded the boot up with bricks to weigh the car down and then snapped the key in the lock so that the scrapyard couldn't open it to check. And off we went. The scrapyard in question didn't care that two teenagers were bringing in an old banger with zero paperwork. They just weighed it, laughed and gave us thirty-five quid. Happy fucking days. Fifteen quid each and five quid to buy weed.

We stopped at a lad's on route back to the boat to buy weed. We were now on foot, and the time was ticking. We got our weed and then jumped the train back to the docks. We decided that we needed to have a cheeky joint before getting back to the boat. Now, there was, and I believe still is, an old abandoned clock tower at Wellington dock. We used to go there occasionally for a joint whilst attending sea school. It was only around two hundred metres away from the boat and clearly visible. The layout consisted of a stone exterior with a spiral staircase and a doorframe at the top, as the door itself was missing. Inside the door frame was a large hexagon-shaped room. A few of the floorboards were missing, and believe me, it was a fucking long drop to the bottom if somebody was unfortunate enough to fall through. It was dangerous as fuck. We didn't care at the time anyway. We were stoned and made out of rubber and magic.

On this particular day though, Thomas and I went running up the spiral staircase. We were already running late after our lunchbreak, but we wanted that joint. We got to the top of the staircase, into the doorframe then whoeee. Fuck me. We ran straight into what I can only describe as a surveillance operation. Black netting draped over the open windows. Men dressed in black, wearing balaclavas. Radio equipment. Binoculars, cameras the lot.

Thomas and I just froze. I had the weed deal in my hand. I just dropped it. Thomas just sort of let out a squeaky fart. 'What the fuck are you lads doing up here?' said this fucking huge gorilla of a man. I could ask you lads the same fucking question, I thought. I don't think these are undercover potheads, Paddy lad.

'Erm, we are off that training boat down there, mate. We just got lost.' I said.

'Get yourselves back down to that fucking boat now. You haven't seen us up here. Do you understand?' Arhhhh, I thought. These are official. Where's that weed, Paddy? Oh, it's by your foot. Tie your lace quick. DOOFA.

I goes down, picks up the weed whilst fumbling with my lace at the same time. Then, 'Okay, thanks, bye.' Out we goes. Like fucking lightning down the spiral staircase. Now, running away, up or down a spiral staircase, is so fucking frustrating, because the object you are trying to escape from stays right next to you until you reach the bottom or the top. Anyway. We gets back onto the boat. We then got all the lads out onto the deck and started pointing up at this building, right at the gorillas. The surveillance team must have thought, those cheeky little bastards.

They did do me a good turn to be fair. I tied in this story to Ian, who believed that his car had been confiscated by the S.A.S., and he paid me my fifty pounds the next day.

So sorry, Ian. I was joking about the piggy bank. I would have preferred notes to be honest. Never mind. Oh. I do believe that engine noise was your tappets too, mate.

CHAPTER 7
Setting sail

Sea school was now over. Now here comes the test. Your first ship, Paddy lad. Luckily for me, my first ship, the *Serenell*, a fifteen hundred gross ton general cargo coasting vessel, was docked in the port of Garston, Liverpool. It was only around twenty minutes' drive from my home. I remember the occasion like it was yesterday. My dad, nan and my two baby brothers came along to see me off. Fuck knows how we all fitted in my dad's Lada Riva 1.3 litre GL. A truly horrible-looking car. A car without curves, should we say. Looked like the design of the car that had been the result from the winning entry of a five-year-old's draw a car competition. Still stuck in the Cold War USSR fucking flowery wallpaper era. A bit like the owner's underpants to be fair.

We gets to the ship, and my dad takes me up the gangway. 'This way, son.' Yeah Dad, I thought. A bit too fucking obvious that – there's only one way to get on. Unless you've got a trampoline in your pocket. Have you been reading my nautical course notes? ten out of ten, Papa. He introduces me to the captain as if he is a fucking crew member himself. It's okay, Dad. I can take it from here. I might be stoned, but I am not fucking mute.

The captain. Brian Smith. An actual real nice guy to be honest. He wasn't what I was expecting to see though. I had visions in my head that he would somehow be in full uniform, with a cap, a big white beard and holding a massive tray of fish fingers. Off-piste again here, sorry people. I've got to share this. A mate of mine has a girlfriend. Lovely girl she is. She is a proper fucking Highlander ginger though and bright copper. Anyway, she went to the fanny barbers for one of those Brazilians, you know, that stripe sort of thing. Anyway, that evening they were in bed. He was stoned and I think she was; I wasn't there so I can't clarify that. Anyway, they decided to have a game of mummies and daddies. Pin the tail on the donkey. Whatever the fuck you want to call it. So he said to me a few days later, 'Yano what, Paddy, it freaked me out. I pulled her knickers down and I thought it was a fucking fishfinger.' It still makes me laugh now because he was so serious.

Anyway, let's get back on track. So Captain Brian Smith. Dressed as if he were on safari, with his khaki shorts and massive knee-length socks with brown sandals. He puts out a hand to me. Oh, this must be the adult fist pump. I shook his hand and we exchanged pleasantries. My dad pulled him to one side and gave him the old political, 'This is my son. I am delivering him here in this condition. He comes back in the same condition, or me and you, Brian, are going to have a problem. And that includes his arsehole,' talks. Then my dad goes back down the gangway and joins the rest of the family on the quayside, already waving goodbye to me.

The fucking boat wasn't even moving. Why are they going over the top with the waving? You're glad to see the back of me, you bastards, I thought. Into the car they all get. Still overkill on the waving and then fucking big wheel spin. My dad's off, handbraking around the corner as if he was thinking, I need to put some distance between us and that little bastard. No, I am just kidding, they didn't. They just stayed there. Still. I think they are still there now, to this day, I haven't checked. No, they drove away slowly, blowing kisses and all the lovely stuff.

Then boom. I was all alone. An odd sort of feeling came over me. I can't describe it. Homesick. I hadn't even sailed a metre yet and I was sick of this job. I couldn't throw the towel in again. Not after all the effort I had put in with my maths lessons. I just wanted to go home. Now, little did I know, the reason everybody came to see me off is because they were all heading straight to the airport, onto a plane and emigrating to Canada. With no forwarding address. Fuck me, this felt strange. I couldn't understand it. Emotions were meant to be unattached when I was stoned. But this was something different. I needed another joint.

Anyhow, Captain Safari says to me, 'Patrick. The vessel is departing for Ternuzian, Holland, tomorrow. If you like you can go home again tonight and come back in the morning. Would you like a sub?' Hang on. Back the fuck up a bit there, Brian. Far too many words and noises have just left your lips there for my tiny brain to process. Holland. Yes, I like that. Home again tonight. Yes that sounds good too. Sub? What the fuck's a sub? I was thinking. Surely not a submarine? Why would I want one of them? The plan was to be on top of the water, not under it.

'Oh yeah,' I said. 'Thanks. What's a sub?'

'An advance. Cash,' he said.

'Oh yeah. Definitely, thanks,' I said. So I started to take off my clothes.

'Put your clothes back on, Patrick'. Sorry, people. Even now at forty-five years of age, I can't help what pops into my head. It keeps me amused.

So, Captain Fantastic wants to give me money and take me to Holland tomorrow. What a fucking cruise. I like this now. That afternoon, I jumped on the bus to Thomas's house. He hadn't been sponsored for his ship yet, although he actually joined the same company as I did a month or so later. He and I just got fucked up, wasted, that afternoon. Sitting out in the sun, talking about how excited I was going to Holland on the ship. I was excited deep down, but equally I was a bit scared. The ship. The crew. One of the seamen looked a bit like Quasimodo, but without the hump. One eye where the eye should be and another by his chin. He creeped me out at first, although he actually turned out to be a great bloke and helped me through some really tough emotional times. A bit like a dad. But an ugly one. The kind of guy that you would keep his picture on the mantelpiece to keep the kids away from the fire.

So that evening, I went back to the ship and into my cabin. I locked the door. Six extra pairs of underpants on for protection. Looking back, I should have just taken a pair of my dad's with me. They would have turned the fuckin Trojan army around, them things. Fuck that, Spartacus. That is an enemy not worth sacrificing our empire for, sire. They are barbarians, savages, formidable and ruthless little creatures. You can smell their evil from lands afar, across the oceans. Even the gods fear their presence. Just a massive line of my dad's undies just standing to attention, steam all around them, growling. No mercy. Grrrrrrr. The Roman soldiers just looking at each other in disgust. Hands covering their mouths, some in tears, weeping like babies. The front line just a sea of vomit. No fucking way are we touching those things. Retreat. Save yourselves.

I actually sobbed that night. Why did I feel like this? Probably because I had smoked the last of my weed. Fuck knows.

Six months later, after sailing all over Europe, the vessel came back into Liverpool. I was originally only supposed to be doing a three-month trip, but I loved it once the homesickness had passed. I had had a great six months thus far, hopping from port to port, going ashore with the crew for a few beers and humping the shite out of any girl that was up for it. I had become a man. Scratching my arse and rubbing my testicles when I got out of bed. A hard-working and proud man. I now had confidence whilst sober.

I hadn't mentioned to my parents that the vessel was in Liverpool. I just wanted to surprise them and just turn up at the door like a fucking castaway. However, first I had to take myself to the hospital. Why? Well, let's just say that my humping around Europe had left me with a bit of an itchy cock. The crew of my boat had, as they all bragged, had many doses before in their careers. So, they were able to put me on the right path as to whom I needed to see to get it sorted.

So, with that, I took myself to the Royal Hospital in Liverpool. I went straight up to the reception desk. 'Excuse me there, sweetheart. Whereabouts is the special clinic in here?' I said, with a cheeky little grin. In my fucked up head she would be thinking, ohh, this sexy bastard in front of me must have a dose. Which means he must be experienced. A man of the world. I must give him my telephone number. What a catch. When in fact she was probably thinking, get away from my desk, you horrid little boy.

Anyway, I was swiftly directed to the clinic. First, an assessment from a rather attractive nurse. 'Right. Patrick. I have a few questions. Now, some of these you may find a bit personal. However, please be as honest as you possibly can, as it's really important.'

'Yeah, no worries love, fire away,' I said.

'Okay, Patrick. When was the last time that you had sex?'

'Erm, about two weeks ago.'

'Okay, Patrick. And was that with a regular partner?'

'Nope.' Joking, aren't you, petal, I thought. Look at me, I'm a heartthrob.

'Okay, Patrick. And where was that?'

'Erm, in an alleyway, I think.'

'No, Patrick. What I mean is, what area? Was it local?'

'Oh no, it was in Spain.'

'And did you use protection at all, Patrick'?

'Tut, no, did I fuck.'

'Hmmm, okay, Patrick. Now, before that. When was the last sexual encounter?'

'Erm, about two weeks before that.'

'And where was that, Patrick?'

'Germany.'

'Okay. And was that with a regular partner?'

'Nope.' A cheeky little wink in her direction.

'Okayyy, Patrick. And did you use protection there?' This went on until she either ran out of paper, ink or patience. Then it was off to the bed for a physical examination. Three female nurses. All with the white coats on. A variety of pens and spectacles poking out of their top pockets. Yeah, Paddy lad, just like a porno, this. Just whip the old cock out, lay back on the bed and go to that happy place. I fucking wish. They stabbed my purple-headed womb ferret right in the fucking eye. Made me scream like a girl, it did. I've never had issues since. Note to all you male readers. Stick a balaclava on the bastard when in new territory. You can't get a prosthetic cock on the NHS. Note to all the female readers. Yeah. Aren't I a catch, eh? Forty-five years of driving experience behind this fit arse.

After the cock carnage, I jumped into a taxi and headed home to see the family. I had a weird sort of feeling in my man sausage, as if it was somehow angrily shouting at me, 'There was no fucking need for that, Paddy lad. Seventeen years, Paddy. Seventeen fucking years you have kept me safe and secure, tucked in snugly between the bollocks and what do you do? You let those three psychotic fucking bitches prod and poke at me. I just don't know what to say, Paddy, I really don't. Why, Paddy? Why? I need answers.' Shut the fuck up, cock. Have a day off, for fuck's sake. I can't have you in my head when I'm hugging me mum.

So I got home. Stepped out of the cab. I noticed all of the windows on my parents' house were all boarded up. A steel frame on the door with a 'SOLD' sign stuck on it. A gust of wind blew a coil of tumbleweed across my feet. All of the neighbours' doors and windows just slammed shut. There were ants running up the walls, looking for cover. Rats head-diving into the sewers below.

I headed into the house and saw my family. Loads of hugs and kisses. Tell us this and tell us that. Then I was off again. Another three months. Nine months in total on my first vessel before I came home on leave. I did this job for around four years, working my way up the ranks, from trainee deckhand to able seaman, or category one seaman, as it's officially titled. The highest grade a seaman can go. After this, I got a job on a fast ferry from Liverpool to Dublin. The *SuperSeaCat*. This is when it all started going tits up for Paddy.

CHAPTER 8
The first stripe

So, I got a position as a seaman on the *SuperSeaCat* fast ferry, or a craftsman, as the job title was. I was thinking, craftsman? I can't even put a fucking curtain rail up. It was, to be fair, a good job. I was twenty to twenty-one years of age and on a decent wage. The shifts were four days on and four days off, both on day and night shifts respectively. There was no accommodation for crew to live aboard the vessel, so once your shift was completed, another team took over and you went home. There was a good bit of transparency aboard. I liked that. Passengers, hustle and bustle, and the stewardesses were a nice added bonus. All lovely girls too.

Within the first month, I was called up to face the captain for a disciplinary hearing for verbally abusing a passenger. Now, picture this. The ship had eight hundred seats for passengers. They were all arranged, sort of like an aircraft, all facing forward. The ship was one hundred and twenty metres long, and as well as accommodating eight hundred passengers, it also accommodated one hundred and eighty medium-sized cars. So not the biggest of ferries but big enough.

On this particular day, the boat was virtually empty. We were on the return crossing back to Liverpool when this fucking gobshite of a passenger, who was sitting in a seat right next to a ventilation intake, started complaining that his legs were cold. The gobshite in question saw me standing at the on-board shop, talking to one of the stewardesses behind the counter. Now, I was easily identifiable as crew because I had a radio, or walkie-talkie, clipped to my belt. I don't know why they call them walkie-talkies either, you know. They work just as well when you stand still.

Anyway, he came over to me and said, 'Young man, can you contact the captain on your walkie-talkie and ask him to switch off the ventilation over there?' and pointed to the seat that he had just came from.

Now, already I don't like this prick. 'Why, what's the problem?' I said.

'It's that bloody ventilation over there. It's blowing cold air all over my legs.'

I just looked around at all the empty seats and shouted, right in his face, 'Well, fucking move seats then, dickhead.' I couldn't help myself. I just haven't got the time for morons. Anyhow, that little incident put old Paddy right on the fucking radar.

The drugs had stopped at this point. I hadn't had any at all for well over three years. Drink was now my thing. I didn't drink to excess, really I didn't. It was all nice and controlled. I always had money in my pocket. A few pints every now and again, and that was that. Then, what pops its head into my life? Charlie. Or to give it its true name, cocaine.

I was in my local pub, The County Arms, in Walton, Liverpool, where I lived. I was in there on this particular night, together with my mate from the ferry, Paul. We were just having a few pints and playing pool. Then, a lad whom I knew well, and still do, Anthony, came over to me and started chatting away. 'Hey, Paddy, how's tricks, mate? Do you fancy a line?' Now, instantly I knew what he meant. I was half-pissed anyway.

'Oh, I don't know, Anthony. I've never tried it before,' I said.

'Yeah, no dramas, Paddy lad, it's up to you, mate'. Hmmmm, this has got me thinking now. Oh, fuck it. What's the worst that can happen? Why not.

'Yeah, go on then, Anthony.' So I followed Anthony into the shitter. He then racks up this big fat line of cocaine on the toilet shelf and then hands me a rolled-up note.

'Just one big, hard sniff up the nostril, Paddy,' he said. Shumfff. Like Henry the Fucking Hoover. Straight up the nose.

'Nice one, Anthony lad,' I said. Then I was back out of the shitter and back over to the pool table. I then took out a cigarette from my pocket and lit it. That's just how I roll, people. Fucking hell, I thought. I feel. Erm. Fucking nice here. This guy, this stranger, then came over to me and asked me if I had a spare cigarette. 'Why, mate? Haven't you got any smokes? Wait there, buddy,' I said. Fucking buddy, I said to myself. I've never said that word in my life. Fucking nice word though, I like it.

So I ran out of the pub and over the road to a newsagents. 'Erm, erm, twenty ciggies, please, my mate; erm, erm, a lighter and, erm, two packets of chewing gum please, buddy.' I was hopping from one foot to the other. Fucking hell. I feel great here. 'Eh, mate, I fucking like your shop. You sell loads of stuff and that, don't you? Fucking bog rolls, Pot Noodles the lot. Good on you, mate. I hope it all works out for you. There you go, old buddy of mine. There's twenty quid. Keep the change. Get your kids some cola cubes or some shit, pal.'

Fucking pal. Where're these words coming from, Paddy? I don't know, Paddy, but they are fucking nice words. I love them. And I love you too, Paddy, I said to myself. Ahhhh, thanks, Paddy. I then ran back over the road, nearly getting knocked over by a car. Beep. 'Whoops, sorry, bud. My mistake. Lovely fucking car by the way.' I went back into the pub and over to the stranger. 'There you go, my old mucker. I got you a packet of smokes, a lighter and a packet of chewing gum. If you don't want the chewing gum, just give it to your kids, my mate. Say it's from Paddy. Proper juicy fruit them too, mate. Not the cheap knock-off shit.'

The guy just looked at me as if I had two heads. He took the gifts, said thanks and just walked away. 'He is a fucking nice feller, him, you know, Anthony,' I said.

'Do you know him, Paddy?' said Anthony.

'No, mate, just met him. But he just seems like a nice down-to-earth gent. The kind of man you could trust looking after your dog whilst you went in the shop.' Fuck me, I was everyone's mate. I loved everyone. I even bought the dog, Sheba, a family bucket of chicken from the KFC on the way home. She just looked at me like, 'Ahhhh, thanks, Paddy mate.' I patted her head. I will chuck your collar in the washing machine for you, girl and buy you a new kennel tomorrow. Enjoy your chicken. Love you.

That was me hooked. Slowly at first. Every weekend. Then it increased to every time that I had a drink, I would want a line too. The drink was just no longer enough. The price of cocaine versus habit is relative to the individual, i.e., the occasional user can sort of afford, or manage, the cost. My habit/addiction ratio however, as I already knew, was off the fucking scale. The consequence analysis. Or the little I had gained in those three years of sobriety was back out of the ears. I just fucking loved the drug. I felt like a superhero. Mary fucking Poppins. See a pigeon cutting about outside a shop. I would go in to that shop and buy that pigeon a loaf of bread. I loved everything. I wanted it. I wanted it bad.

Did I have the money for my habit though? No, did I fuck. Right, Paddy lad, I said to myself. Do you remember when you had that side to you that would lie and cheat and do whatever it took to get what you wanted? Yup. Good man. Get that cunt front and centre now. We have got work to do.

CHAPTER 9
Meeting the one and only

So there I was, just yearning for that feeling of euphoria constantly. At whatever the cost. I purchased a car on finance from a company on Scotty Road, near me. It was a green L-registration Ford Mondeo. With a credit card thrown into the bargain. It was a lovely car and pretty new at that time. I felt fucking great. I was on this lovely planet, and I was cutting about on this lovely planet in my lovely car, snorting copious amounts of lovely cocaine. Truth be told, I should never have had the car to begin with. Why? Well, I didn't have a fucking driving licence for a start and therefore no insurance either. But I didn't care. I deserved it. The law doesn't apply to you, Paddy lad. It's not a risk, because your subconscious doesn't do risk management any more. All the law wants, Paddy, is for you to be happy. So just carry on. Paddy's Law. The only law.

It was becoming a problem with my parents too. They didn't want me cutting about the streets noon and night in a car, illegally. Fuck what they think anyway. Fuck everybody. I will do what I want to do. Because, if I don't, then what's the fucking point? Well said, Paddy. That deserves another line of the white stuff. My nostrils would be arguing with each other, the left one kicking off on the right one. 'Eh, you had the last line, you greedy bastard.' Calm the fuck down, nostrils. Tut-tut, you two. There's plenty to go around.

One night, I had been out to a club called the Montrose. I was together with my mate, Paul. We were both standing by the dancefloor at ten to two in the morning, ten minutes before the DJ finished, just before the lights come on and the club closed. We were in that desperate state. Must get a girl. C'mon. Make eye contact with one, Paddy, for fuck's sake. I don't care what she looks like. As long as her name's not fucking Mad Bob from the Dingle, fucking hairy legs and a five o'clock shadow.

Finally, we both homed in on these two girls who were also looking desperate too, funnily enough. We left the club and all boarded the Mondeo. A cheeky line of charlie off our thumbs to quell the travel sickness ahead. Kids these days key it – I mean, they stick their keys into the product and snort off the end of that key. What tit thought of that idea? The way I snorted in those days, I would have lost the fucking key. A locksmith would have had to try and retrieve it through my ear or some shit. Kids these days, eh. Braindead little bastards. I blame the parents. Most of them are braindead bastards too.

Anyway, I said, 'Girls, are you two to up for a fucking massive party then or what?'

'Yeah, too right we are, whoop whoop whoop!' screamed Barbara. Right down my bastard ear. Any more of that nonsense, Barbara my little snowdrop, and you will be fucking walking. I don't think her name was Barbara either. I made that up.

Soo, mirror, signal and manoeuvre, checking my blind spot for cyclists, and we were off. 'Paul,' I whispered. 'Will your mum be in bed? Can we take them back to yours?'

'I don't know, Paddy, we can check. No music on though. We will just have to put the telly on dead low.' Good stuff. So I was driving like a bit of a spanner, showing off really, trying to get the ladies to the ball on time, this once-in-a-lifetime illegal rave when, like the knob that I was, I drove past a police station, in a 30mph zone, at around 70mph, just as these two squad cars were leaving the station. Oh fuck. Nee-nor-nee-nor-nee-nor, blue lights once again. I pulled over. The officer opened my door. He then took one look at the state of me, my fucking jaw swinging side-to-side, bouncing off the steering wheel, reeking of fucking Red Stripe lager. You're nicked, son. No keys back this time, Paddy lad.

In those days, the police didn't have the resources to check people's driving licence status and insurance details, etc. So it was just a case of being banged up for the night until I sobered up. The next morning, an officer came to my cell. 'Have you got a full driving licence and insurance?'

'Yeah, of course I have.'

'Okay,' he said. 'Off you go.' I then signed out of custody. I was given back my keys and informed that my car was parked around the back and that I would hear in due course about a court date. A summons.

I then left the station, and who was waiting outside for me? My good mate Paul, fully kitted out in police tactical uniform. 'I've been undercover, Paddy. We have been trying to get you for years.' No, I am joking; he was in his craftsman uniform. Shit. We were due in work in an hour or so.

'I hope you have got a big fat fucking line for me, mate? How did you get on with them two girls last night? Spill the beans,' I said.

'Oh, my mum woke up and kicked them out. I had to walk them around the corner and put them in a taxi.' So, both of our nights had been ruined. What's this world coming to?

I was out with Paul a couple of weeks later. We were in another club, a club where I met the only woman I have ever truly loved. And still do. Not in a creepy bastard way. She is the mother of my equally beautiful and super-intelligent daughter. She was out with her mate, Gill. I remember the night like it was yesterday. She was dressed in this little black dress. An hourglass figure with fifteen minutes thrown into the bargain and a fucking huge nose. No, kidding. She looked, and still does look, stunning and is beautiful in every way. Her cooking was fucking awful though. Jeezzzus. I lost some weight with that girl.

I fell for her instantly, and she felt the same way. She couldn't keep her hands off me in fact. I can't really blame her for that, she is only human. The problem was, though, that nose. I just couldn't let it go. No, the problem was, I had this habit, which, looking back, she obviously knew about, but somehow she could see through it. What a fucking roller coaster ride I was about to put this this poor girl, Emma, on.

I never cheated once on Emma throughout our relationship. I didn't need to. Look what I had on my arm. I was, however, a flirty bastard, to the point where I would drive for three miles, every shift, in the opposite direction from my home to pick up two stewardesses for work and then drop them back home once finished. One particular day, it was snowing, and icy, and a little bit dodgy on the road. This would have been a few weeks after meeting Emma. So I got up out of bed that morning. I was a little late but I could make that up. I had my usual vitamin C, right up my fucking nose and into the car to got to get the girls for work.

I had hardly had any sleep for days. I had just been snorting my brains out twenty-four-seven, trying to reach a level that I was never going to reach. That's the thing about drugs. Any drug. You reach a peak and level out. The drug cannot get you any higher than you already are. But you truly believe that it can if you continue to take more and more. That's when overdose creeps into the room. Anyway, I picked up the girls. I was sliding all over the road, struggling to keep control at the speed I was driving. I never wore a seatbelt back then. It wasn't good for the image. Lads liked to give the impression that their heads exiting the windscreen at 50mph wasn't such an issue. Ah, it's okay. I've always got a box of plasters in the glove box.

On this particular morning though, due to the car, or should I say due to the way I was driving the car, causing it to slide about, the stewardess, Diane, lovely girl, was nagging at me. 'Paddy, please put your seatbelt on.' So I did. We eventually got to work, onto the boat and completed our shift. After that shift, we got back into the car. The snow and ice had cleared by then, and it was a nice, sunny early evening.

Now, the only thing in my head was Charlie, Charlie, Charlie. I needed a fucking line. I felt fucking awful. Rough. Coming down. So these two stewardesses were in the car with me, and to be quite honest they were getting on my fucking nerves. Yap yap yaperty fucking yap. All happy and yapping. You know what? I am going to just put on my seatbelt, because I can't be bothered listening to Diane fucking nagging at me again. I just wished that at that time fucking James Bond ejector seats were an optional extra in the Ford Mondeo package, because these two girls would have been orbited in seconds.

So, mirror, signal, manoeuvre. Checking my blind spots for cyclists, I pulled away safely and blended in with the traffic. All I could hear inside my head was Charlie, Charlie, Charlie. It was getting louder and louder. So I pulled over, and this guy came up to my window and said, 'Oh, I do beg your pardon. I thought you were Charlie.' The girls were still giving it the yap, yap, yaperty, hahaha, yap, yap, outside my head. Fuck fucking me, I was thinking. These two are like social fucking vampires. I can feel them sucking the fucking life out of me. I need a cigarette. So I pushed in the cigarette lighter (kids, just google it) and leaned my head forward and down into the lighter to light my smoke.

Suddenly, I saw this beautiful white heavenly figure coming towards me. It was covered in light-blue cloud and whispery curls of smoke. What was this heavenly figure, Paddy? My fucking airbag. BANG. Right in the bastard face. I had gone straight through a red light and into the side of a car. I pushed this car a good twenty metres sideways, I reckon, with the impact. The car was a five series BMW and was carrying, guess who? A fucking solicitor. Thank God there were no kids involved and I was wearing a seatbelt, otherwise I would have been sharing my story via a séance.

I looked at the girls. There was horror on their faces; they were shocked but not badly hurt. At least it shut them up. I tried to get out of my door, but the front of my car had been pushed back over the door frame. So, I had to jump out of the back door. I then went running over to check on the car I had just hit. Now somehow, my arm, upon impact, had hit something, either the door or wheel, I don't know. Possibly even the airbag. However, the result was that my arm was stuck up in the air, as if I was about to throw a punch.

So I ran over to this guy that I had just sideswiped and whose day I had basically ruined. He saw me running at him with my arm up and fist clenched and assumed I was going to batter shite out of him. Either that or he thought it was a kidnap attempt. Anyway, the poor fucker is cowering in his car. I banged on the smashed window, which was a bit pointless, but I didn't notice at the time. I shouted at him, 'Are you okay, mate?' Anyway, he soon realised that he was in no danger from me, so he climbed out of his passenger side. I then ran back to my car and put my head inside the window. Silence. Perfect. That was one good thing to come out of this.

I then spotted a phone box over the road, so I ran over into the phone box, threw on a pair of red undies and a red cape and just fucked off. No, I made a phone call. I was in the phone box already so I thought I may as well. I then ran back to the scene of the accident. (It was accident back then. Now, through political correctness bullshit, it's known as a traffic incident, simply because the word accident implies there is no one to blame. Wouldn't you think the prick that named it 'accident' in the first place would have checked the dictionary for the meaning of the word before applying it? Wanker.) Anyway, when I got back, the guy I had hit said to me, 'Was that the police that you have just called?'

'No,' I said. 'It was my mum.' He just looked at me like, you fucking dickhead.

The sum total of all of the above was me attending court (the first appearance of many) on charges of drink driving, no licence, no insurance, driving whilst intoxicated and reckless driving and telling porkies to the Plod. Two words they don't like there. Pork and Plod. Arhhhh, toughen up, snowflakes. Sticks and stones, boys. Sticks and stones. Turn up at your door dressed like fucking Robocop. Mr Bennett, we are trying to ascertain the events leading up to blah blah fuckin blah. Drop the textbooks, dickhead. You are really a true wordsmith, officer, so intelligent. Let's not go down that route, eh? I will leave you standing from the off, looking all confused. Speak to me like a person and we might get somewhere. Do you go home after your shift, open the freezer and speak to your fishcakes like that? I am trying to ascertain whether to have you with chips or mash? You probably do to be fair. Taser your fucking mash to heat it up. I will deal with you shortly, fishcake, and process you shortly, pea. Hahaha aren't I so funny. No; bore off, get a sense of humour, you fucking robot. Plebs.

That's not all of them, by the way. A lot are sound. The rest need fucking drowning. What's the selection process like for the matrix division? One question, officer: are you a cunt? 'Yes, I am.' Welcome aboard. Here is an extra truncheon. Now you can go bully two people at once. Hearts and minds, people. It pisses me off watching these programmes such as *Police Interceptors*. They flash the profile of the officer in question on the screen like a Mortal Combat avatar. PC John Stafford. Twenty-seven years on the force. Likes Pot Noodles and *Strictly Come Dancing*. Favourite car: Aston Martin DB9.

Let's break this down, eh. Firstly, no one gives a fuck. Only idiots laugh at shite like that. The mere fact that PC John Stafford is still only a PC after twenty-seven years on the force says to me that this fucker isn't too bright. He can't even climb up the ranks to sergeant. The fact he that likes Pot Noodles, which incidentally so do I, but it's not on my CV because it's irrelevant. And the fact that he likes *Strictly Come Fucking Dancing*. Which I don't. But again, it's relevant. Why do you think this make him appear cool? It makes him sound like a bigger knobhead in my eyes. He is dumb, his nutrition intake is all wrong and he is a fan of Dorothy, and he has a poster of a car on his bedroom wall like a twelve-year-old boy.

Now, PC John Stafford. Twenty-seven years as a PC because he likes the action and doesn't want to make it to the rank of a sergeant because he doesn't want to sit behind a desk. Likes dressing up as Darth Vader whilst wanking off to goat porn. Loves a skateboard and Scooby Doo. Now that's something I would laugh at. Fuck fucking me. Enough of that shite anyway. Let's move on.

It was my first offence, anyway, or the first I had been caught for, should I say. So the sentence was a fine and a ban on my provisional. When I eventually got one. The M.I.B. (not the men in black, kids), the Motor Insurance Branch, dealt with the financial impact. Now my lovely Mondeo, or the three quarters of it that was left, was thrown onto the back of a flatbed truck and then landed on a friend's driveway. The car was finally assessed and declared as repairable by a fucking genius of a body specialist.

The cost was an issue though. Fifteen hundred pounds all in. There was no way I was going to be able to pay for this myself. Not with my habit. So my dad fronted the money for me. I remember him giving me the money. 'Take this down to the mechanic's workshop, son. The car is nearly finished, so pay the guy and he will drop the car of here in a couple of days. Now, it's a lot of money to be carrying around, that, son. I've asked a pair of my underpants, fresh off the front line, to go along with you for protection.'

'Thanks, Dad,' I said. So seven hundred and fifty pounds went to the mechanic that afternoon, with the promise to pay him the rest in a week or so. Which never happened. The other seven hundred and fifty was divided equally between the two nostrils.

I came home a couple of weeks later, after a night shift. It had been raining. I was expecting to see my Mondeo parked outside my parents' house as I turned the corner. However, there was just a dry Mondeo-shaped patch. My car had just been freshly stolen. I had been the victim of a crime. Me. How bloody well dare they? Common criminals. I was truly and utterly appalled and traumatised. This Paddy lad required copious amounts of vitamin coke to overcome the trauma. I felt wounded. I cried myself to sleep that morning, I don't want to walk any more. I don't think I can go on like this. Sob, sob, sob. My dad's underpants came into the bedroom. 'Oi, dickhead, tone it the fuck down, otherwise I will come in here and sit on your face when you're asleep. ALL RIGHT.'

Things went downhill fairly rapidly from there. The cocaine had its grip firmly upon me. I was scheming day and night to get what I needed. Manipulating people. I was getting noticed a bit more on the ferry too. Not just for my dashing good looks but because I was acting like a bit of a prick to be honest, barking at people, jumping up at them and licking their faces. I was always late for my shift too. My heart just wasn't in it any more.

One time, in the early hours in the morning, I was fucked and totally exhausted. As mentioned earlier (if you have bothered to pay attention), there was no accommodation on that vessel for the crew. Therefore, there was nowhere to get a little cheeky nap. Fuck this, I thought. I am dead on my fucking feet here. I need to find a hole or something to crawl into or I am going to just drop. I was drained, both mentally and physically. The product of my scheming had taken its toll on my brain. You have exhausted all options here, Paddy lad. You need to recharge those vital brain cells and start making plans.

So with that said, I went looking for a hole, a den, if you will. There were three steel lockers in the bow, or front (the pointy end of the boat, kids), on the car deck. These things had just been built, or erected, for storage purposes. They were approximately ten feet by ten each, enough for me to stretch out in and get a little snooze. So I went to check these things out. Two of them were padlocked. The third one had a padlock on it, albeit not secured. Boom, nice one. So I opened the door and looked inside. There were just a few of those sort of changing room steel lockers inside and nothing else. This will do nicely, Paddy lad, I thought.

I sat down and leaned my back against one of the lockers, a

little bit too hard, and one the doors on the top popped open, causing this little box to fall out and land on my bastard head. Ouch, ye fucker, I thought, what was that? So I picked up this little box. Guess what was in it? Go on. Guess. Okay, I will tell you. It was a box of perfume, or cologne. I can't remember which, but it was good stuff. Not the shite that you buy from a Romanian car wash. This was the real McCoy. What the fuck, I thought. I bounced up in shock, as if I had accidently sat on a cock, and opened the locker door fully. Fuck me, it was full of these things. The next locker was the same.

'HOUSE,' I shouted. Fucking bingo, Paddy lad. Another mate of mine, Dozy Dave, was on the same shift as me. He too was a bit of a lad, although all of his disposable income went on kitting out his camper van. He loved that thing. Nice little wagon to be fair. (Leave the fucking tent talk, Paddy, what happened? I hear you say.) Well, I reported this directly to the supervisor on shift, who promptly thanked me for my honesty and then locked everything up securely and reprimanded the fool who had left it open in the first place. Did you? No, did I fuck. I was born at night, people. But it wasn't last night.

There was an opportunity to exploit here. So with my new-found energy, and ring sting, I went to find Dave. He was more excited than me. 'Fuck, Paddy,' he said. 'If this is in here, Paddy, then what's behind door number two?'

'Oh, Dave, you might look like a gormless bastard, but I do like the way you are thinking.' We needed to find out so we went to door number two. Shit. 'This padlock is secure, Dave'. Next thing, BANG. Dave just came right behind me and belted this padlock with a 4lb lump hammer, shattering the fucking thing. 'Fucking hell, Dave, you dopey bastard, I dropped my fucking arse all over the floor then,' I shouted. I opened up the door.

Inside was the Holy Grail. Cascaded in heavenly rays of light. Duty-free cigarettes, tobacco, champagne, wines and spirits. Now, apart from Emma and my daughter, and of course my own reflection, it was the most beautiful thing I had ever seen in my life. I dropped to my knees, clasped my hands together, head tilted towards the heavens and wept. Thank you, Lord.

Now, the problem we were facing was that, this padlock, or what was left of it, was going to be discovered once we got back to Liverpool in a couple of hours, if not sooner. So how do we get the merchandise from the boat to the suitcase type of thing without being noticed? We could rule out Dave. One foot in front of another was an overload for him. So I needed to make up a plan. It was time to summon the cunt from my inner mind. Oi, Cunt. Oi, Cunt, wake up. 'YESSssss, Paddy, sniff sniff, I is here. I smells a bit of shiverley in the air, sniff sniff.'

Good, you're awake, Cunt. Now listen. I need you to scan the situation you see in front of you and formulate a plan for me, like fucking ASAP. 'Hmmmm, YESSssss. I am always here for you, Paddeyyyy, sniff sniff. One moment.' My eyeballs then rolled into the back of my head for synchronisation. Then boom. I was back.

'Right Dave,' I said, 'I have a plan.'

There was a large, let's say eight-foot-by-eight, steel bin on wheels on the car deck. This was used for chucking waste cardboard boxes in and shit from the crossings. This bin, upon arrival at Liverpool, would be pushed off the vessel via the car ramp and then up the corresponding ramp and into the terminal car park. It would shortly afterwards be collected by a forklift truck or a bin wagon and emptied. Then it would be pushed back onto the vessel ready for the next crossing.

'Right, Dave. The plan. We grab a couple of boxes of

cigarettes, twenty-five thousand per box, a few boxes of spirits, tobacco and a couple of bin bags full of perfumes. We bury them in that fucking bin, under cover of the cardboard boxes. The stewards, as per usual, will then collect the bin once we dock and push it up the car park. It will obviously weigh a lot more, but like you, Dave, they are a bit dim and simple, so I guess they will evaluate the extra weight as them just being a bit tired or weak, again, Dave, a bit like you.

'I will stand by the car exit ramp as the foot passengers are leaving the boat. I will target some old dear, or old bloke, or somebody that looks like they could do with a helping hand with their luggage. I then, as the nice, handsome, caring sort of chap I am, will offer to carry their bags for them and chaperone them up to the car park. I then, whilst whistling innocently, going about my business, will push the bin and its contents over to your camper van.

'I will then slide open your side door, leap up into the air and bellyflop into the bin. I will then swiftly empty the booty into your van. Volt out of the bin. I will then close your inner curtains to keep nosey bastards at bay. Close the side door, lock it and then kick the bin in the arse to clear it away from the van. I will then gazelle it back to the boat as if I have a lion hanging off my arse. Back on board. Job's a goodun. Safe and secure.'

'Fucking hell, Paddy,' he said. 'Did you rehearse that?'

'No, Dave. Let's just say the force is strong with this one, my mate.'

The operation went down to a T. As if it were executed by the great S.A.S. themselves. It was flawless. Exact. Not suspicious in the slightest. Shortly afterwards, I was returning my radio to the charging points located on the command bridge. It suddenly started going fucking bananas. I could see stewards and stewardesses running around, shouting at each other on the car ramps. The captain, who was also on the bridge, was on the internal telephone giving it the old, 'What, how, where, when' shit. I thought, oh, fucking shit, here we go.

The First Officer, who had his car on board, went flying off the car ramp like fucking Herbie and straight up to the car park. I could see him stopping right next to Dave's van. He then got out of his car, and I could see him peering through the back windows. I've already covered that angle, you prick, I thought. But hang on. How did he know it would be Dave and me? That's a stupid fucking question, Paddy lad, I answered myself. Your plan has gone well and truly fucking south here, cunt, you wanker. What are we going to do? 'Paddddeyyysss, sniff sniff, I must now rest. I am weakened and tired. I must SLEEP, SLEEP, SLEEP, SLEEP, SLEEP, SLEEP… My eyeballs then rolled back into my head and de-synchronised. He had fucked off, the bastard.

I legged it down to the car deck to find Dave. He looked shocked, almost looking as if he had just been given a prostate examination with E.T's phone home finger. 'Dave. Snap out of it, you dozy bastard. Give me your van keys again. I've got to get that van and its contents the fuck out of dodge.'

He handed me his keys just as the First Officer appeared. 'Oi, you two,' he shouted. 'I fucking know it was you.'

'Who the fuck are you calling Oi? You fucking gobshite. Don't speak to me like that ever again. I don't know what you are talking about,' I shouted back.

'Well, the police are on their way.' Shit. I had no other option. It was now or never. Where was that fucking lion? 'Here, kitty kitty.' Off I went. Fucking Mach 6 up the ramp, breaking the sound barrier as I went supersonic. Boom boom.

I jumped into the camper van, fired it up and slammed it into what I thought was reverse. Bang. Right into the metal railing in front of me. Shit. Try again. Bang. Could I fucking get it to go backwards? Has this fucking thing even got a reverse gear, I was thinking. In the end I just gave up. I jumped out of the van and shouted to a couple of passengers who were just watching me, looking confused. 'Give us a fucking push backwards, please, lads. Gear issues.' They helped me push it back just enough for me to get full lock on the wheels and then beep beep. I was gone.

It would usually take me fifteen minutes average, depending on traffic, to reach where I lived. I did it in five. I pulled up at a location where I knew the bounty would be safe, slid open the door and offloaded it, cracking open a bottle of vodka and chinning a few swigs to try to get some stability on the adrenalin. Then it was back to the boat, via a petrol station so I could purchase a prop. I got back on the vessel.

Poor Dave still looked like he was still getting finger-blasted by E.T. 'Dave, chill the fuck out, will you. I know it's hard but for fuck's sake, try and take that gormless fucking look off your face'. The police still hadn't arrived, or rather I didn't see them.

Then the First Officer appeared again. 'Oi, where the fuck have you just been?' he shouted.

'I fucking dare you to call me Oi again. Go on, I fucking dare you. You fucking gobshite. I have been to the twenty-four-hour garage for cigarettes, you prick. Knock the Miss-Marple-fucking-Columbo shit on the head, will you?' I held up my prop. Twenty fresh, an unopened packet of cigarettes. Without the legend 'DUTY FREE' printed on them and with a receipt of purchase in my pocket. 'Now fuck off.' I knew at that point that my job was well and truly fucked. I didn't care though, looking back. I was living day to day, not planning my career.

Shortly after that, our shift finished. Dave and I then headed up to the car park. Dave then spotted the front of his pride and joy. 'Oh, for fuck,s sake, Paddy. Have you hit something?'

'Yeah, Dave, I did. About a dozen fucking times, mate. I was like a fucking moth burning its bastard arse on a light bulb trying to get away from that gate. Don't worry, mate, we have plenty of coin in the purse for minor repairs. Would you care to join me for a cigar, David? A big fat line of vitamin C and a wee tipple?'

'Fuck the wee tipple, Paddy lad, I need a fucking bottle after that.'

It must have been some two weeks after that, the ferry company's board of directors, who incidentally must have attended the same church as Gostin Craft Workshop's board of directors, also decided that I was no longer fit for employment. That was three times now I had been the victim of unfair dismissal. How very uncharitable.

CHAPTER 10
The weakest link

So I am now snorting Vitamin Coke to excess. On a totally different level. When things such as sleeping, eating properly etcetera, those necessities needed to maintain and sustain life, begin to become normal whilst using cocaine to my degree, you know you are fucked. What I mean by that is, I was waking up in the mornings, immediately racking up two big fat lines of coke, one for each of the nostril twins, to try and maintain some peace and harmony between them both.

I would then go and have my breakfast, lunch and dinner. Obviously not in the one sitting; I am talking generally throughout the day. A big fat couple of lines with my evening's Horlicks and then straight to sleep. I was functioning normally, albeit with a wild and out-of-control daily habit. And believe me. I wasn't snorting shite. It was seriously strong cheddar. The kind of product that the man from Del Monte would give two thumbs up to if that was his poison. I wasn't getting any higher. I was however getting lower.

'Paddy,' says the one and only. 'We need to talk.' Oh, fuck me, I thought. Serious talk time. I am getting my P45 here. Binned. She has had enough. 'I'm pregnant,' she said. I can't really describe how I felt when she said this, and I am sorry I cannot share that feeling with you. Simply because it wasn't me. It was some other feller's kid. She had been having an affair behind my back, the cow. No, I'm joking of course. What I mean by that is, it wasn't me. I was false. Living a huge lie. It was a form of narcissism in a way, or narcissistic tendencies. Being a person that wasn't me.

I don't mean an alter ego, that's harmless. Such as a man dressing up as a female and taking on the persona of that female. That's just them playing out that fantasy, their alter ego. Such as Eddie Izzard. Great bloke, amazing achievements with his charity work. Mine was borderline narcissism. I truly believed I was somebody else. I wasn't acting. However, deep down I knew that this was a game changer. I started in a way to fight the cunt within. Paddy lad, you have got to get this together, wrapped up. Somehow.

I had now been unemployed for a few weeks. I had cash from various pies that my grubby little fingers were in all over the place. But the thought of going back to work. People telling me what to do again. Having to keep to a schedule. Did I want this? The nostril brothers would not be happy, that was for sure.

It was then, maybe a week or so after being given this amazing news by Emma, that I was sitting up in my bed. It was early hours. My nose was all blocked up. The nostril twins had fucked off and gone to bed for the evening. Closed the gates behind them. 'No more up here tonight, Paddy lad.' I was again properly fucked up. But in a sort of daze, a trance. Just staring at the wall.

As I remember, I wasn't really thinking about anything in particular. My left arm was slowly becoming warmer. It didn't register at first. I was just in a trance. Slobbering. In another time zone. I slowly diverted my gaze down to my arm. It was covered in blood. My nose had just basically shit itself all over the place. It was in my mouth, dribbling off my chin. Fucking everywhere. Shit. Snap the fuck out of this, Paddy. This is serious. It wasn't a nosebleed as such. It was more of a release. Lock gates opening too early type of thing. I jumped out of bed and started to river dance. It just seemed like the appropriate thing to do. I looked into the mirror. Fuck me, Paddy lad. You look as if you have been scrapping with Freddie fucking Kruger. And won the silver.

Now, I truly believe that everybody is born with a weak link. A sacrificial link, should we say. A sort of safety device installed in each being by Mother Nature herself. The role of this link is to break. Part. As a warning, if you like, that this is on the edge. You are dangling by your fucking pubes on the edge of an infinite drop. If this link breaks, you have got to mend the fucking thing pronto. Because if you don't, then its game over, end of the road, lights out, curtains drawn. You are getting planted or processed into ash. You have to be able to identify and recognise that essential link. That's the key. The best route is to avoid drugs altogether.

Mine had well and truly broken at that point. You need to get this fixed fucking now, Paddy. Prioritise this above all else or you're going to become a statistic in no time at all. A memory. I am going to fucking kill myself. I am going to become a fucking father, for fuck's sake.

A day or so later, I proposed to Emma. Obviously she said yes. Jumping up in the air she was. Throwing her little head everywhere. 'Calm down, Emma, love. The baby will think you're in a rave. Plus, that fucking nose of yours darting around the place like that, Emma. It's got fuck up written all over this scenario.' She eventually chilled out. We went to town and I bought her the engagement ring she wanted. 'Yeah, Emma. It's all about you, isn't it? There's a perfectly good ring there, round shaped and everything. A lovely floral-design pearl inside it for thirty quid. And you have to go and pick out that fucking one. Why, Emma? Why? You need to give me some fucking feedback here love. This is outrageous.' Kidding. It was a lovely ring and she was worth every penny. (I still never got that ring back. Even after she vacated me from the premises. I have only just realised that. An invoice will be heading your way soon, Emma.)

We then spent all of that day together. That night we went to our favourite Chinese restraint for some Chinese food. We were clever kids back then, we knew all the right places. You don't go into chip shop to buy a roll of Sellotape, right? We knew our shit. I am going to fix this. Put it right. I love this girl so much and my little angel inside of her. If that cunt climbs out of that cave inside my head, I will just bite the bullet and swallow a pair of my dad's underpants. How do you like that, cunt, eh? The brown rain descending all around you. The smell of awfulness engulfing you senses, stinging your eyes. My dad's underpants smashing your front door. Smile, here's Undies.

So within that week I got myself another job at sea. This time it was working offshore on PSVs, or platform supply vessels. Basically it's what it says on the tin. Supplying offshore oil and gas and drilling installations with whatever they required. Fuel, water, food, barite, bentonite, mud for drilling, drill pipe. Everything. The rotations were one month on and one month's leave. Paid equally every month. Good, honest, decent money. Paddy lad. We need this. So kisses and cuddles all around. Love you, look after that precious cargo. See you in a month. Then onto a train and off up to Aberdeen to commence another chapter of my life.

CHAPTER 11
I was trained By Harry Potter, you know

So the job had saved my life and subsequently created another one. A life of normality (to a degree). Within a couple of voyages at sea, Emma and I had purchased our first house. A step on the rung of the property ladder. It was a small two-bedroom house that needed a lot of work doing to it to get it up to our standards. Emma was heavily pregnant at this stage, her belly sticking out almost as much as her nose. The plan was to have this ready to move into by the time our baby was born. We did however miss that timed window but moved in not long after.

My dad offered to do the building work for us, and I was to assist. I didn't have many skills back then. But I was good at painting and shit and moving stuff about. Labouring, if you like. The man who makes the tea for the man who makes the coffee type of thing. Emma's dad, Rob, another great bloke, was also throwing his hand in with me, lugging stuff about, although like me, he was low in the skills department. So essentially the both of us became my dad's bitches. It was a real joint effort from both families. East meets West.

I fucking love this life, I would think. The new me. Family guy. I was having the occasional cheeky pint or two now and then. No vit C required. Fuck me, Paddy lad, you have smashed the arse out of this. Well done you. It carried on like this for a few years. Still doing my trips away to sea as my rotations dictated. Spending loads of time with my two beautiful girls.

My little baby girl Amy. I was a house husband when I was

on leave. Emma worked for a bank and still does. She would wake up in the mornings. 'Paddy,' she would say. 'You know I love you. But do you really have to sit in that rocking chair all night staring at me, playing Donkey Kong and singing nursery rhymes to me? It creeps me out.' She would get out of the bed as soon as my hand started to wander. 'Off, now,' she would command. Straight into the shower; it didn't matter how cold the house was. Spotless she was.

I would get up behind her, sometimes in front. I would then head downstairs. Heat up the house. We didn't have central heating back then. I haven't got it now either, to be fair. I have one of those water tank heaters. How 1970s urban council house is that? I would make us a coffee and then make her packed lunch for work. Sandwiches. A bit of salad on them, but the cucumber had to be wrapped up separately because she didn't like the way it made her bread soggy. She wasn't demanding at all, to be fair. I loved it though. I would then head back upstairs to get my little angel from her crib.

She never cried much at all, Amy, as a baby. Swore a lot though. I would look into her crib. She would just be lying there. Staring into space, smiling. A bit like Dave Snail. But a beautiful version and without the cock of course. She would see me coming and start giggling and then say, 'Where's my fucking breakfast, Papa?' I would take her downstairs. Change her nappy. I was hardened to such traumas, thanks to my dad's undies. I would then plonk her in her baby walker and she would be off. Banging and bumping into anything in her way.

She would come into the kitchen as I was making her breakfast. Crabbing sideways in her walker. Looking at me with her cheeky little face. Then, for no reason at all, she would just run backwards and slam into the door, her head flying back and

72

forth upon impact. 'A bit of whiplash there, baby girl.' I remember we had this three-CD multi-changing stereo unit downstairs. It was all hi-tech then, believe me. I would often find pieces of toast rammed into the tape deck or the buttons stuck with jam after one of Amy's curiosity calls. I think I will just play a bit of toast, Dad. Doesn't work like that, baby girl. Try a bit of Jam, I like them.

One night, we were all tucked up in bed. Sort of silly o'clockish. The only things out and about outside at that time where police and burglars. Anyway. Emma wakes me up. 'Paddy. Paddy, wake up,' she whispered.

'What's up, Emma? Are we there yet?'

'SShhhush, dickhead. There is someone downstairs.'

'Who?' I said, all confused.

'Erm, I don't know, Paddy, I haven't really been down to check, you knob.'

'All right. For fuck's sake. No need to be sarcastic.' So I got out of bed, my cock thumping on the floor. Shit. I wonder if they heard that? Silence. Emma, I thought, this had better not be a wind up. I can't sleep, so let's annoy Paddy. Then I heard it. Talking. Right, I am in fucking stealth mode now. I throws my cock over my shoulder, grabs a couple of pre-prepared ice lolly sticks and heads out of the bedroom. As I am creeping down the stairs I can hear them whispering.

Now, don't forget. I am still half-asleep and naked. I felt a bit vulnerable and not very scary. Then my head starts giving me those questions that you don't need in a situation like this. Paddy. What if the burglars are gay? Fuck that. I am not wrestling with a gay man. Nude. What if he wins? And he hasn't had his hole for weeks? A bit of spit-roasting with this here one, Barry, I think. Let's make a fucking kebab out of this have-a-go bitch. Shit, they would take turns if they were both gay. Paddy. Get a fucking grip. Concentrate. So I crept forward, and then the voice reached the clarity level. Fuck me, these are talking about aliens and planets and shit. They're fuckin lunatics. Fuck this.

I spun around and straight back into bed. 'Fuck that, Emma. They can take the three-CD hi-tech multi-changing unit with built-in bass boost and graphic equaliser remote display.' Then I heard it. Music. Amy, you little shit. You have just nearly killed your dad off. What had happened? On one of her curiosity tours in her walker, she had somehow, with toast, jam and a bit of witchcraft, programmed the fucking system to come on at that time. The CD she had (deniably) selected was *War of the Worlds*. Jeff Wayne's masterpiece. It begins with a voiceover. The fucking aliens and then the soundtrack. 'I am taking the bastard wheels off that baby walker tomorrow, Emma. Can't we just get one of those seat things? Just hang her up on the door and let her bounce about?'

I will give you a little tip here, people. A lot of good, hard-working, honest people keep some type of weapon in their bedrooms; I do. My dad leaves them lying all around the house. Angry bastards. Anyway. Quite rightly so. I am not condoning violence as a matter of course. But if some horrid, rat-fuck burglar is audacious and cheeky enough to break into your home and put yourself and your family at risk, then in my eyes, the weapon is justified. In the eyes of the law it is also justified. Depending upon certain factors of course. Such as, what type of weapon is used, and whether or not you are actually at risk.

A couple of examples. If you are the type of person who yearns for violence, and upon hearing that glass break, the window lock popping, you spring out of bed all excited and run downstairs as if it's Christmas morning and you're ten years of age, armed with a baseball bat. If that burglar hears you running down the stairs and is trying to escape back out of the window, and you then drag him back into the house and start hitting home runs with his head, then you have fucked it. You are going into bracelets. If the intruder is outside of your property, and you chase him halfway down the street, swipe his legs and then start hitting home runs, you have fucked it. You are going into bracelets.

If you are, for example, a fucking flake, somebody who sleeps with the lights on and is scared of spiders, and you hear that noise, but you are too scared to investigate, so you just sit up in the bed, trying to take your mind to that special happy place, phone in hand with your mum on speed dial, if the burglar then comes into your bedroom and you chuck a fucking throwing star at him or fire a bazooka at the cunt, you have fucked it, and guess what? Bracelets.

The force used and/or the weapon used by you must be proportionate to the force and/or threat that is being applied to you. Gun to a swordfight scenario, if you like. You have the gun, the instant equaliser in this situation. But you are at fault. In this country anyway. You have to really think this through. In the latter scenarios, the average person will panic a bit, if you like. Pumped up with adrenalin. Logic is superseded by these emotions and you could inadvertently do something that, at the time, you believe to be correct. But on reflection, you well and truly went over the top.

So, tip of the century for home defence. You heard it from Paddy first, right? Beside your bed you should have a small box. Or use a drawer if you're the minimalistic, fucking OCD type of annoying twat who gets annoyed with the toothpaste lid being left open. This box or drawer should contain the following: one x pair of lacy, sexy knickers; one x pair of black nylon stockings; one x rubber mask; one x dog collar with matching lead attached; one x golf ball and finally, one x Anal Annihilator Mark Two strap-on rubber cock.

Upon hearing that suspicious noise in the wee hours, you should then. calmly and casually get out of bed, get dressed in your knickers, tights, mask, collar and lead, strap on the old Anal Annihilator Mark Two, throw the golf ball in your mouth and just casually go to find the intruders to work out the problem, knowing that you are not breaking any laws as of yet. Now. I don't care how fucking hard an intruder thinks he is. If that comes towards you, I guarantee you would fucking run. You certainly wouldn't want to fight it. I know I wouldn't. Worst case scenario, you can whip the cock off and batter the fucking shite out of them with it. 'It's just a rubber cock, Officer. It was all I had to hand.'

'Okay, sir, we shall leave that there.'

Did you read about the two burglars in America a couple of years ago? These two poor bastards broke into the home of one of America's most prolific gay male rapists. He caught them red-handed and tied them up. He then just bummed the fucking shite out of them for days. Ouch, ye bastard.

So, I am loving this new life of mine. The new me. One of the officers from the vessel I was working on at that time had only just recently qualified for that rank. His name was, and I presume still is, Harry Potter. Now, the name is bad enough to hold as your title. However, I really feel sorry for this guy, because his original name was Bartholomew Potter. He didn't like this name for obvious reasons. So he changed it to Harry. Some years later, the wonder boy wizard was created. Now, can you imagine how fucking pissed off he must have been when that speccy little prick popped onto the radar?

Harry however was getting me interested in becoming just more than a seaman. 'Paddy,' he said. 'With them hips, you could become a dancing seaman.' Harry had made his way up the ranks, like myself, to a navigator. That doesn't happen much. Especially these days. Most junior officers come from the cadetships route. They have very little knowledge of how the deck works and how a ship operates. Why? Because they haven't worked the deck and don't understand it.

All they know, or want to know, is how to operate the bridge systems to propel the vessel forwards or backwards from A to B. There are very few skill sets installed in junior officers these days. They are not interested. They want to go to the party but refuse to clean up after themselves type of thing. Apologies again, people, for going off on one a bit there. It just fucks me off. Seamanship is a dying passion these days. Especially for these technological generation ignorant little pricks.

Anyway, the thing about Harry that intrigued me was that he sounded and looked like a proper dumb fuck. Obviously he wasn't because it takes a lot of brain matter, combined with the ability of application, to make it to the rank that he had made it to. But he couldn't have always had this knowledge and ability. So I latched onto this, with the outlook of, well, if he can do it, then so can I.

Harry's way of teaching me was fucking epic. Tailored for me. Back to nursery basically. 'First lesson, Paddy. Breast-feeding. I will whip a nipple out and you throw your lips on it and pretend it's an ice pop.' 'Right, Paddy. Algebra?' What did he say then, I thought. Honestly. That was the first time I had heard that word. Or probably I had heard it but not registered it. 'X and Y, Paddy.' Oh, fuck off, I thought. I want to go home. How could I understand what he was trying to teach me if I didn't understand what he is saying?

'Paddy, listen. Bill has eight pence and Jack has four pence. Bill is X and Jack is Y. Now, how much must Bill give to Jack so that they have the same amount of money?' I just looked at him. Was he taking the fucking piss? How was I supposed to work that out without a calculator? Right from the fucking start, point dot, he taught me, and I was getting it. Absorbing it like a sponge. More importantly, I liked it. Loved it, in fact. I understood it. Get me a pencil and a fucking notepad because I am off to watch Countdown. Step aside, Carol, you dumb bitch.

I was the same with trigonometry, which is the basis of chartwork, map reading. Charts are based upon WGS 84 for datum. What is this, Paddy? World Geodetic Survey. The last one was conducted in 1984. Hence the title. It's a mathematical representation of the earth taken from its global shape and flattened out for the purpose of navigation. The subtle differences between the shapes of a globe versus a sphere. Why it's so important to get them right. I was loving all this. Lapping it up.

'Okay, Harry, ask me another one.'

'Okay, Paddy. This time, Jack has the eight pence and Bill has the four. So how much has Jack to give to Bill?'

'Fuck, you got me there, Harry. Ask me one about motorbikes.'

Really, I was smashing the fucking arse out of this. Me. An officer. That would make my two girls proud of me. They were my inspiration. My reasons. I wanted this for the three of us. I needed this.

I was given sponsorship by the company I was working for at that time. They paid for everything. Fifteen months of intense training in nautical college in Fleetwood. I actually met David Jason there, the great Del Boy from *Only Fools*. He was filming an episode of *A Touch of Frost* in Fleetwood and was using the pool on site for a scene. They showed him around the campus, where I ended up driving a computer boat with him. Nice guy. Fucking legend. They kept me on full salary. They even arranged a chauffeur to collect me and drop me off at the train station when I went home for the weekends. I would go shopping of a weekend with my two girls. I would walk around the supermarket, fucking Terminator behind the eyes. Just green lines running up and down, left to right behind my eyes. Scanning everything. I would scan the price of a tin of tuna. Look left and scan the price of a packet of poppadoms. Divide the sum total by that tin of rice pudding over there, Paddy. Next.

A couple of years after Potter, I qualified as an officer. I thought I would have to adapt the way I spoke. Start using words like 'Yar', 'Oh, absolutely, yes', 'Fantastic effort all around', 'Spiffing', 'Bravo'. I never did though. I just sound like a sarcastic bastard using words like that. My tongue tries to catch such words as they leave my mouth. None of that fucking nonsense exits on these here lips. Paddy lad.

This officer. Family guy life continued for a time. We still had our little issues in life as every family does. But it was fucking awesome on the whole. I loved life back then. Holidays away in caravans. Abroad in Turkey. Just me and my two girls. I had made it. I still didn't have a driving licence for a car yet though.

Unfortunately this wasn't to last. Why? Well, another drug popped into my life. A drug powerful enough to turn my head inside out. Amphetamines. Speed.

CHAPTER 12
Getting up to speed

We had moved up on the property ladder. Sold our first house and bought another. A massive semi-detached place, this was. It had a huge living room, which opened up onto a huge dining room. There were patio doors leading onto to a massive garden at the back with my own tree right at the rear of the garden. Together with my man shed. Beautiful fitted kitchen. A lovely-sized front entrance with banister staircase leading up to three large bedrooms upstairs, plus a fitted bathroom. A driveway at the front for our family car. I even had a driving licence now. A real one.

It was already done up to a fantastic spec. All we had to do was move in our luggage. We loved it, we really did. Everybody in the street just seemed so nice. Emma's sister. Trisha and her husband, Lee, lived just over the road together with their two kids, James and Rebeca. A lovely family. It was all good. I had become friendly with a lad who lived a couple of doors away from our previous property. This lad, Kevin (who sadly lost his life in a motorcycle accident during the Isle of Man TT races, R.I.P. Kev), was a dealer of amphetamines, speed. Not on a massive scale. He predominately sold to friends and a few others. Just to fund his own habit, basically.

Now, speed. Amphetamines. The drug that changed my world. It's a horrible, dirty drug that devastated everything I had. I had always, prior to this, viewed the drug as scummy. Up there with heroin in a way, and it is in some cases. Especially with me. It doesn't have the physical withdrawal that heroin has, whereby your body and mind are screaming out for it. Cramping you up, shitting your pants even at the mere suggestion of letting out a fart. It makes you want to cry, or die, or both. I have never had this experience myself with heroin. But I have been around many heroin addicts in prison and places and witnessed this first-hand. It's not nice, and I can sympathise with them to a degree.

Speed on the other hand has more of a mental withdrawal. Your brain wants it. The physical side, in comparison to heroin, is non-comparable. You just simply sleep, a lot, to catch up with the deficit of sleep you lost due to days and nights of trying to invent shit without a rest.

One of, if not the, greatest inventions of all time. The wheel. You can't improve it. It just works. Okay, we have adapted the way wheels move over time with buffers, springs and bearings and such things. But the design itself. It's perfect. Amphetamines and speed make you look at that wheel and think, you know what? That's a second-rate invention. I can do better.

It all started for me, at first, the same as any other drug. Slow. It was fucking cheap too, relative to the amount I was taking at that time. It's fucking great, I thought. I am just on a constant high. Fixing stuff that isn't broken. Seriously. The extremes that you can push your body and mind to whilst on that drug are phenomenal. I would often stay awake for three to four days. Flat out, just tampering away with stuff. Taking stuff apart, just to see how it worked. Then putting it back together, albeit with around fifteen screws, four wires and ten springs left over.

I would look at the object once I had re-built it, thinking, I wonder where all these bits left over came from? Obviously it didn't need them in in the first place. Let's plug it in to test it. BANG. The fucking thing's blown up. It must have had a fault already. I know. The toaster looks like it could do with a yearly service. Let's dismantle that fucker. Deep clean that toaster, Paddy. Don't just shake the crumbs out like a normal person. Three hours later. Oh fuck it. We have got a grill anyway. I will just keep the toaster spare parts to make a circus for gerbils if we ever get any.

Every fucking thing I would dismantle. Nothing was safe. If Emma and Amy were made from screws and bolts I would have dismantled them too. Amy cutting about in the street playing with her pram, sporting a leg three times bigger than the other, with a fucking huge nose. Emma finally able to get closer to the mirror without a telescope. Sporting Amy's nose. The ideas that used to pop into my head were mental. Although amazingly creative and Golden Globe-merited in my eyes.

Right, Paddy. Let's surprise the family whilst they are sleeping. Take of all the doors in the house. Re-hinge them at the top, so that they open like a gull-wing door on a supercar. No one else has doors like that, Paddy (probably because the person following the one in front would be smacked in the fucking face with a door, you tit). Nooo, I have thought of that. Fit a slow-closing piston to them. So that they close slow, nice and controlled. Maybe rig them up to a smoke machine, so that when you open the doors, smoke emits from the bottom, thus giving the impression you are entering or departing a U.F.O. I will have to calculate, by means of calculation, just how much smoke is emitted, because restricting the visibility in this house could be dangerous. Emma coming around the corner in the fog, at speed. Some poor fucker coming the other way is going to lose an eye. The family will love it. Where's my chainsaw?

Honestly. I would fuck everything I touched. I did learn a lot, in a way. But the cost wasn't worth the cause. I remember this one time. My lovely sister Lea-Anne. That's how her name is actually spelt, by the way. Unique or what? It was actually a product of my dad being himself. My sister was born. My dad went to register the birth. 'Lea-Anne', he wrote on the birth certificate. 'Excuse me, Mr Bennett,' says the lady registrar, 'that's not how you spell that name.'

'Listen, sweetheart. She is my fucking daughter. If I want to call her Frank, I will. Now just counter-sign it, and we will forget that we ever had this conversation. Do you understand, love? I know your husband, he is very fond of his legs. Let's just keep it that way, eh. There's a good girl.'

Anyway. She found this old black-and-white TV in her loft. 'Oh, I will take that, sis. I will get that working. Maybe rig it up to an alarm device so that it switches itself on in the morning and wakes you up. Maybe boil you an egg too.' My dad is a sort of jack of all trades. I asked him for his diagnosis. 'Eh, dad. What are your thoughts on the status of this TV? You know. Just give it to me straight. One technician to another.'

'Throw it in the fucking skip, son. You drive boats. I fix shit. Don't mess about with stuff you don't understand.' Not the prognosis I was expecting, Father. I will show you my talents. I built a kaleidoscope last week out of two kitchen roll tubes and an old pair of spectacles, I will have you know.

So I gets this TV. Plonks it on top of our lovely dining room table. Emma and her sister Trish watching me from the living room. Paddy, you have an audience here. Lay an electrical wiring diagram out next to the TV, colour bits in with Amy's felt-tip pens. Various colours. They will think you're a fucking genius. Lift up the diagram next to the circuit board as if comparing the two and say things like, 'Oh, no. No no no. This is all wrong. The voltage can't possibly emit the correct amperage through that logic gate. It needs a potentiometer in sequence with two resistors to stand half a chance of survival. Tut, tut, tut, Hitachi, eh. Must have been a late Friday night job, this one, girls? Hahaha. Oh, my giddy aunt.'

I takes this thing apart. Drops one of the circuit boards out. Simply blew the dust away inside. Then I plugs it in. Switches it on and BINGO. The fucking thing just fires up into life. YESSssss, Paddy, you fucking genius, I was thinking. Now I am sitting at this table, nursing a fucking massive semi. Emma's probably sitting there now thinking, Paddy. Oh my man is so clever. I will have to crack the old suspenders out tonight and treat him. What a hero. In fact, upon reflection she is probably thinking, you have scratched that table, you dickhead.

So, re-assembly time. I unplugged the TV (I'm not an idiot) and then grabbed the circuit board to slot it in place. BZZZZZZZzzzzzz. Fuck, I'm being electrocuted. But it's not plugged in, Paddy. This is fucking VOODOO. Then release. Fuck me. That didn't look cool. What had happened was, the capacitors (electrical components on a circuit board), their primary role, other than filtering, is to store electricity and hold that electricity once the power is switched off. For low voltage applications such as timers and memory, or RAM as it's now called. These were working, that was for sure. They discharge their stored energy once a bridge is made between the anode and the cathode, or plus and minus, if you like. In this case, the plus was my left hand and the minus was my right. The bridge was through my head. I felt as if I had just been tasered. Hair sticking up as if just freshly combed with a toffee apple. I never learned though. First shock of many.

It carried on like this for a good while. I was still going back to sea for my month's voyages. However, this became more like rehab. I was joining the boats on a fucking high. Then a couple of days later, no drugs. The comedown. Sleep deficit as mentioned earlier, it catches up with you in a big way. You could literally sleep standing up. Absolutely fucked for days. The thing is, I was still in command of this huge ship for twelve hours a day. Driving it alongside oil and gas platforms, with high-pressure gas risers all around me. If I hit one of them, the fucking rig and its three hundred persons on board, or P.O.B., would go up in flames. I would be famous for all the wrong reasons.

Was it upsetting me what I was doing to my family? Of fucking course it was. Once the drug wore off, I would go through all of the heartache. I hated myself for what I was putting my two girls through. They didn't ask for any of this. They didn't deserve this. All Emma wants is me. Paddy. All Amy wants is me, her dad. Is it so fucking hard, Paddy? Unfortunately, at that time, yes it was. Some say I favoured the drugs over my family. I wanted the drug more than them. Well, fuck you for thinking that, you ignorant bastards. Drawing conclusions on the basis of your own ignorance to understand the condition. Don't piss in my pocket and tell me it's raining. It's all about the switchboard, the layout. Having the tools necessary to apply the logic. I couldn't at that time fully understand risk and consequence. I do now. I have paid the ultimate price for this knowledge.

CHAPTER 13
Did I kill him?

I joined a vessel in Aberdeen. High as a motherfucking kite again. I should have been there some hours earlier. But me being me, the ignorant I am. It's my shout, this. I am the First Officer. The fucking boat can wait for me. It can't go anywhere without me anyway. I was just so fucking cocky, as per the drug's effects on my persona. 'Oi, you. Oi, you, yeah, you with the fucking dressing gown on and the daft beard. Fucking Roses or Moses. Whatever your fucking name is. You see that Red Sea that your parting there? Well, it looks like hard work, that, Moe, my old snowdrop, to be fair. Fair fucking play to you, lad. Just keep it parted like that though until I am ready to cross. When I am ready, in my time. Good trick by the way, Moe. You will have to share that secret with me. If you show me how to part seas and shit, I will show you how to make a miniature Victorian lamppost out of a pen, a torch bulb and an AAA battery.'

I got to the boat in my hire car. Parked up the car and left the keys on the back wheel as instructed. I walked over to the vessel and up to the gangway. I met an A.B. (Able-bodied Seaman). Thinking about this now as I am writing, it should be A.B.S., shouldn't it? Anyway, this A.B. greets me. 'Hello, sir. You must be the new chief,' he said.

'Oh yar, that's me, peasant, greetings. I won't shake your hand, pleb. I don't know where you have been. Tuck that shirt in and stand up straight when you address me, you little fool of a man. Now, be the good slave and fetch my shotgun and polo sticks from the Land Rover. WELL. Run along.'

I said something along the lines of, 'Yeah, that's me. Paddy. Nice to meet you.' We shook hands.

'My name is Indie. We are running a bit late, Paddy, I think.'

'Yep, I am well aware of that, Indie. Okay. Get the lads together. Do a quick toolbox talk. Get the gangway in and single up on all lines. Please let me know when this is done. I am going to prepare for departure at my end.'

That was it. I didn't feel too bad to be fair. Just full of my own self-importance. I heads up to the bridge. The captain is standing there. He puts his hand out to greet me. 'Ah, you must be Paddy. Finally made it. My name is Terry. I am the captain.' The fucking uniform sort of gives that away, Terrence, my old petal, I thought. He must have been bottom of the class in nautical school, this cunt at spot-the-rank lessons.

'Okay, Terrence. Do you want to give me a quick induction up here? Show me what buttons and associates need manipulating to get this girl moving?' I am not a naturally cocky person, now people. I am actually very polite and well-mannered, impartial and sensitive to indifference. However. On that drug I am a nightmare. Like one of those gobshite American rappers. America's got fucking Ten Bob. 50 Cent. Liverpool's got me. The full quid.

So we departs the harbour. Straight into a fucking gale of wind with matching seas. I could do with that Roses feller here now, I thought. The ship is dancing that dance. Like a horse when you burn its arse with a ciggy, just fucking everywhere. Loop the loops, barrel rolls, the lot. I took the first watch. The first six hours. I would have taken the first six days if I had to. I was wired to the moon. Although I did only have a little bit of speed left. Enough for one more hit. Fuck, I wished I had brought more. My subconscious never let me take drugs to sea. I think the reason consisted of two main factors. The first being, deep down I wanted to sort my shit out and go home to my girls as me. Paddy the partner and Paddy the father. The other factor was that the drug doesn't lend itself to the conditions the sea and a ship bring with it. I guess it takes the drug plus freedom for the experience to be worth it for me.

Anyhow, so we are getting our fucking heads kicked in on this boat, in this confused seaway. Now, this A.B., Indie, was on watch together with me. He was my lookout. His primary role was to look out of the windows and search for target vessels' lights, and/or the corresponding aspects of such vessels. He then should report them to me, whereby I could then cross-check the bearing and approximate range/distance with the radar and see if I had acquired that target, thus giving me feedback such as CRS (the course of the target), SPD (the speed of the target), CPA (the closest point of approach of that target) and BCR (the bow cross range, if applicable).

I could then determine if a risk of collision and/or a close quarters situation existed with that target vessel. I could then act accordingly, as per the international regulations for the prevention of collision at sea, or rules of the road as we mariners call it, and so on and so forth. The latter sounds a bit robotic. The exchange of information is a lot more formal than this, but I am just trying to give you an understanding of what the situation was. Basically, he was my third and fourth eye. Co-pilot, if you like, and therefore he had to be switched on to his game and give me correct feedback so that I could identify and work the problem in good time, should one exist.

Indie however had come from very large vessels, VLCCs (Very Large Crude Oil Carriers). These things are fucking huge.

So big, in fact, that a lot of them carry petrol scooters just to get from the stern to the bow, or the back to the front (kids, the blunt end to the pointy end). The motion of these very large vessels in rough seas is totally different to the offshore vessels I served on and still do. They roll and pitch a lot more slowly and methodically. The vessel we were on at this time rolled and pitched very quickly in comparison. Like a buckaroo.

Indie, the poor guy, wasn't used to the motion in the ocean on a smaller vessel like this and subsequently was seasick. I could see this as soon as we departed Aberdeen. He went from perky, chatty and full of conversation to pale, sweaty and fucking mute. Seasickness is horrible, it really is. I have only had it the once in my life, but once is enough. He was at this point a dead weight to the watch. He could not operate at the level required to maintain a safe watch. So with that said, I told him to leave the bridge, send me up another A.B. in his place and then go and lay down in his cabin and rest.

Some twelve hours later or thereabouts, after taking my six hours rest period off watch and dismantling half of the electrical appliances in my cabin, I was back on duty. The boat was still shaking that booty all over the fucking place, smashing herself into the seas ahead, letting Neptune know she was up for the fight. I said to the duty lookout, 'How's the patient? Has he surfaced from his bed yet?' We were laughing about it. Although we all know as mariners that seasickness is awful, we still take the piss out of crew that suffer. Just because we can. It's all in jest and good humour.

'Paddy, he looks really fucking bad, you know. He is like a fucking zombie, and he hasn't stopped throwing up.' Okay. Now, although I may have still been a bit wired myself, I did recognise that I had a duty of care to my crew. Safety of my crew first, safety of the vessel second. The end. I called Terry on the internal comms.

'Captain, can you please come to the bridge and take command whilst I go and check on the status of Indie?'

'Yes, Paddy, no problem, I am on my way'. Terry then took the command and I went down below to the accommodation and on to Indie's cabin. As soon as I opened his cabin door, the smell of vomit was fucking awful. He was just lying in his bed, baulking. No fluids coming out of his mouth, just retching violently.

'Right, lads, get the medic and get him down to the hospital now,' I said. So, we did. We laid him down on the hospital bed. The medic was now checking him over.

'Paddy,' he said. 'His temperature is off the fucking scale here. We need to get him stripped off.' So, we did. Next thing, this poor guy just bolts upright on the bed. His eyes just looked three times their normal size. Then bang. He just hit the pillow with his head. Fuck me. What's just happened then, I thought. It was a mad and odd moment. Everyone was just looking around at each other, confused. Then it kicked in. Get the fucking defib now.

The defibs, or defibrillators (the heart-shocking unit), that we use at sea are similar to those that you see in shopping centres, etcetera. They are called A.E.D.s (Automatic Electrical Defibrillators). Now, unlike the ones used in hospitals that will deliver a shock at the doctor's command, these things don't. They will deliver the required amount of joules at the required timings through their own inner algorithms by way of monitoring the casualty's heart beating status. Basically, you cannot force them into shocking the casualty if the computer says no.

There is a subtle difference between a heart attack and a

cardiac arrest. The difference is simple. When you watch in the movies, the machine in the hospital that's monitoring the heart, it's making that beep noise. You see the green peaks, or spikes, on the screen. And then the line flatlines and the machine sort of goes beeeeeeeeeeeeeeeee. If it flatlines shortly after a peak/spike, then that's a cardiac arrest. The heart has just stopped. Fibrillation is limited. Now, a heart attack on the other hand will act differently. Back to the green peaks/spikes on that screen.

When the heart goes into attack, it will fibrillate, vibrate. It loses its natural rhythm between the two peaks, or beats. It will not flatline immediately. The green line on the screen will become wavy, zigzagged, progressively getting less wavy over a short period until it does eventually flatline. That's what these A.E.D. machines are searching for. The unnatural rhythm of the heart. The vibration. From the moment the heart comes from that spike/peak to the zigzags and then goes flat. That is the only window of opportunity you have for these machines to work. That's why you need to get those two pads hooked up to the patient's torso fucking pronto. To allow the machine to do its thing.

Unfortunately for Indie, he had suffered a cardiac arrest. The heart had just stopped. Apart from thumping on his chest, there was nothing we could do to try and shock his heart into starting up again. We were too late hooking up the pads. The poor guy was in his thirties with a young family at home. He passed on a fucking boat, in a fucking storm, surrounded by amateur medics. What were his last thoughts?

The other issue we were facing now was legal. As amateur medics, we were not allowed to declare the death. We had to continue working on him until a doctor and/or a professional medic called it. This happened around an hour later, when the coastguard winched a doctor down to our vessel by helicopter. Amazing people, these coastguard teams too. I have all the time in the world for these guys.

Anyway. For an hour, we took turns with chest compressions and rescue breaths. Fifteen-two was the ratio for chest compressions back then. Fifteen compressions to two rescue breaths. It was fucking heart-breaking. Watching the lads, in a sort of queue. Waiting silently take their turn to work on this poor guy, who we knew was well and truly gone. The doctor, when he stepped into the hospital, realised the pain in the room. He administered a shot of adrenalin into Indie, albeit orally into the mouth due to all his veins collapsing, as a way of saying, I suppose, you did your best, lads.

It was the seasickness that was the major factor in his death essentially. That and dehydration. His body just couldn't take the shock. How do I know this? Because it's my job to know this. I am trained to a very high standard in advanced medical care. I can legally administer injections, rig up a catheter and triage multiple casualties by means of a full primary and secondary survey, hand in hand with the Glasgow coma scale. I can treat major burns, infections, shock, bleeding and lacerations and a whole list of others. I am trained to a high standard in firefighting. Search and rescue. Command and control. We do not have the resources at sea on speed dial if it goes tits up, such as the fire brigade and ambulance service.

We must deal with these situations ourselves accordingly, dynamically, through our training and experience. A lot of people think my job is easy. And it is, ninety-nine percent of the time, if not more. They think I just sit in a chair, looking out of the windows, dodging boats, drinking coffee and ordering crew about. No. That's what you think you see. I am paid for what I know. Not for what I can do. What is inside of my head. What I can bring to the party when it all starts to go tits up. That one percent, when you want the man in front of you to know his game and how to play it. It's called leadership.

Well then, Paddy. If you know so much then, and if you had not been wired to the moon, would you have saved him? Maybe yes, maybe no. I don't believe I would have acted any differently whatsoever at that time, whatever state or condition I was in. It was standard practice and still is. If somebody is sea-sick, you get them to lay down. That's all they wish to do anyway. Have I learned from it? Yes, I have. I have learned a lot and carried these lessons forward. Now I don't hesitate to call in the coastguard for support and CASEVAC a casualty off the vessel.

I did this recently with Captain Donald Haggart. Legend of a bloke. We treated him on board accordingly initially, but I was straight onto the coastguard to get him off the vessel at sea. He went on to receive emergency heart surgery that day. His life was saved. Yemmi, a Nigerian geologist working on my vessel in 2015, east of Africa in the Mozambique Channel. She became seasick, whilst pregnant, I later found out. I practically forced fluids into her and ensured that a crew member was at her bedside, monitoring her every minute. It messed my head up quite a lot, this situation with poor Indie. Mainly because of the hour or so we had to spend working on him after his passing. That and nagging doubts of failing his family on my part. I was young.

We turned the vessel back around and headed back into Aberdeen. Indie had been laid in a body bag and airlifted onto the chopper. The mood on board was fucked up. Just fucked up. I was now on a major comedown. Exhausted, confused, depressed. I felt as if I couldn't stay on the vessel any longer. We were interviewed by the authorities individually to gather facts and rule out foul play. I then jumped back into a hire car and headed home again. Only this time, I had had enough. Fuck the sea. Fuck that job. I just want to get fucked up and forget about the whole lot of this.

CHAPTER 14
The milkman

I have witnessed a few people lose their lives in front of my eyes on this journey of my life. I've witnessed mates losing fingers, hands, falling and breaking their backs, never to walk again. Shitting into bags for the rest of their lives. In operations I was directly involved in. And two that I was in charge of. One poor guy was crushed to death just a couple of feet away from me. The noises around him and the noise he was making in his final seconds have never left me. The eye contact between the both of us. I just looked on, powerless to help. Michael Tarrager. So sorry, Mike. God rest your soul, mate.

Another guy, on a particular New Year's morning, slipped on a ladder and fell between the ship and the quayside. Again, this guy had passed by the time we recovered him back to the vessel. However, again CPR and the associates still had to be maintained until the professionals arrived. Paul Abington. R.I.P., Paul. So sorry, mate. James Perrot. Thirty years of age. A real, true friend of mine, James was. His beautiful wife, Macy, pregnant with their first child. You were a fucking legend, James. R.I.P., mate. Please feel free to pay James a tribute on his Facebook memorial page.

I have never shared these events with anybody really. I've spoken about them to friends when I have been on a different planet, where up there it's acceptable for me to talk about them. Plus the occasional psychotherapist, who truly believed they had cracked the mystery, the aura surrounding Paddy when I opened up like this. No, you prick, back up. I shared this with you because you asked me to. You didn't find it. Post-traumatic stress, or P.T.S.D is a real thing. It does exist, believe me. Creeping up on you when you are at your lowest. Why? Because it's a cunt, and that's what a cunt does.

Certain noises make the hairs on my neck stand up sometimes. I don't know why; it doesn't even have to be a noise relating to any trauma. Just a noise. I don't wake up sweating in the night or any mad shite like that, or have nightmares. Although I did have a nightmare a couple of years ago that a fucking washing machine was chasing me around the streets. A fucking washing machine. I know. Mental, eh? Every fucking house I escaped into, this bastard thing would just appear. How the fuck does a washing machine get upstairs on its own? It must be the ghost of all the washing machines I have disembowelled over the years whilst trying to install a new gearing spin system in them. Propelled by an army of hamsters in balls connected to belts and pulleys. Yeah, people. That's the future.

What I am getting at is that this disorder doesn't only exist in the services. Doctors, nurses, medics, coastguards, firefighters, military personnel and police (to a degree). They are the real and true heroes in all of this. They see and deal with such things daily, albeit without the emotional connection to that person. However, it does affect Joe Public just as much, and sometimes on a different level. Simply because there is no network of helpful resources or aftercare to follow up with. Of course, after these traumas, the companies I was working for at that time did offer counselling, etcetera. But to me, in my eyes, this was a line filler. Red tape that they had to overcome to fall in line with policys and method statements of caring for our crews. Putting our workforce first, and all that utter bullshit-speak. It's all about the coin, people. If it wasn't, then nobody would have a job.

Anyway, let's back to the nitty fucking gritty. The average and normal individual. Yep, you know who you are. You lucky, disciplined fuckers. They would have, in this situation, gone home. Kissed the Mrs and child. Hugs all around and offloaded to them. Obviously not your child; that would be a wee bit insensitive and perhaps traumatic to that child. Come on, baby, Dad's going to read you a bedtime story. Once upon a time. On a ship… I didn't though. I went straight to a dealer's house. I then changed my emotional state by means of putting myself into a chemically induced coma.

Now I can go home. Just as cocky as ever, make-no-sense Paddy. They will understand that. 'I am fucking finished with the sea, Emma.' No explanation. No reasons why. I am a closed book. Unless you tie me up and tickle my belly button, you are getting no information from me. The same applied to the hire car I had travelled home in. We had our family car. However, I was going to keep hold of the hire car until I was ready for it to be collected. Why? Because I fucking wanted to. It was my right. The company owed me big time for putting me through that ordeal.

The fact of the matter was, though, it was my job, my life. I signed up for this route and was subsequently paid a lot of money for doing it. I didn't have bells and whistles to just chuck about and make noise with on my demand. I had a contract of employment. The words such as, grow the fuck up, Paddy. Get off that fucking pedestal. Stop being selfish. It was all just noise to me. Clutter. Static, cracking on a radio that I would simply re-tune to my own station. It's all about me. Paddy fucking FM. Such words are for the plebs. The mere mortals. Fucking cattle.

Weeks passed. I was just like fucking Rocket Man. Off my fucking cake constantly. I still had this hire car. Parked around the corner. Out of sight. It became my friend. My partner. I would rub its paintwork tenderly and lick its wing mirrors. Tease its exhaust until it backfired. We would go out together on manoeuvres as and when I needed to. Emma didn't know. The family car was parked on the drive. He can't go far, not without a car. He is probably just playing hopscotch in the school playground around the corner.

I needed a plan. I was now taking speed like there was a drought on and backing this up with copious amounts of cocaine. The two drugs don't complement each other in any way. A bit like putting a spoonful of pineapple jelly into a bowl of chicken soup. It's scatty. It sends your head all over the place. A horrible sort of high, weird. (The drugs, I am talking about here, not the pineapple and chicken soup, kids. Get out of the kitchen cupboards.)

However, I just wanted to overtake that kite, soar above it. I needed resetting somehow. I needed to be shocked into giving this up and seeking help. That help was there. Right in front of my fucking eyes. Just there, all that time, arms out ready to catch me. My two beautiful girls. But could I see this through the mist? Nooo. Not at all. I didn't at that time have what it took to recognise this. Or maybe I didn't want to recognise this back then. Fuck knows how my mind worked its thing in those days.

Oi. Cunt. Oi. Fucking cunt. Wake up. 'YEESSsssssssssssss, Paddy.' Sniff sniff. 'A long time, my old friend.' Sniff sniff. Don't call me a fucking friend, you horrible little scumbag. Now listen. Let's have it right. You are a cunt. But you are good at what you do. So, do that voodoo that you do do and find me some fucking finance.

So, I began to flick through the Yellow Pages. (The tactile search engine, kids. A bit like Google. Difference is, you can wipe your arse on this one if you run out of toilet paper.) There, I had found what I was looking for. A violin supplier. Learn to play that fucker and busk for coins. I found a company that manufactured plastic storage containers. What I wanted was twenty-five-litre plastic re-sealable drums. And a few of them. I went to collect these from said manufacturer. It was not too far from my home actually. Fantastic drive, lovely scenery.

So now I had the drums. Now I needed the wood. Then I could build the raft and row to South America and pick up my drugs for a fraction of the price. Everyone's a winner. No. Seriously now. Apologies. I just feel a bit happy and giddy today. All from my own merits too, I will add, no chemicals, except coffee. So, I now had these plastic drums. The hire car I had, that in my eyes was mine now, was a VW Golf. These drums fitted in the boot, standing up fucking perfectly. As if designed for this mission. I did not have to modify the vehicle in any way whatsoever, which was a tad disappointing. I am not sure VW would agree, but there you go.

Now it was time to begin filling up these drums. Filling up the drums? With what, Paddy, I hear you ask. Diesel. Every fucker with a diesel engine needs diesel, right? It's a demand. Taxi drivers. Van drivers. Residential drivers. Not the red or green shite that we use at sea or that the agricultural and farming communities use, high in sulphur and dyed that colour for duty purposes. I am talking pure diesel. From the pump. What pump, Paddy? The pump at the petrol station. What petrol station? Any fucking petrol station that I passed.

Here is how it went down. I would pull into a petrol station, or a fuel station, for those pedantic pricks. Firstly, I would top up the tank on my hire car (let's call that travel expenses). I would then, casually, whilst whistling away, open up the boot and start filling up my twenty-five-litre plastic drums. One by one. The pump cut out at one hundred quid. I would then screw the lids back onto my filled and partially filled containers. I closed the boot, the car and then got into it and just drove off to the next petrol station, where I would then repeat the process until all drums were full. Then I would take out my little black book, and off I went on my rounds. Just like the milkman.

I would go to one of my punter's homes. Or a workplace. One must be flexible in business and attend to one's clients' needs and desires. I would agree a sale price on a container or two. (Prices fluctuated as per the FTSI and share prices in general. I was running a business here. One had to be sensible.) I would then decant a container into the punter's car (I know, what a service) whilst making idle chit-chat, such as, 'What a lovely spring morning, sir. Was it the silver service you were after on this occasion? If you become a member of my exclusive gold service, you will receive such things as a free air freshener with every twenty-five-litre top up and be entered into my monthly raffle to be in with a chance of winning a digitally remastered *ABBA Gold Greatest Hits* treble CD, for your listening pleasure and delectation. This includes all the best hits, such as "Saturday Night Fever", "Once in a Life- time" and my personal favourite, "Dancing Queen".'

I would then whistle the sample tune whilst polishing the paint clean of any spillage. 'Okay, sir. The silver service it is then. There you go, fan-bloody-tastic. All diddly done. That's two twenty-five-litre drums. One decanted and one remaining. The empty drum will be collected by me on Friday. There is a surcharge of five pounds per day, sir, for any twenty-four-hour incursion over the drum rental agreed period. Should you happen to go over this limit? Don't worry too much, sir, I am very friendly with the boss, hahahaha. I am sure I can convince him to, let's say, ease back on that fine a tad, sort of tighten up the reigns slightly, hahahaha. Thank you, sir. You have a nice day now. Safe motoring. Tatty by now.'

I had a client list in no time. I am fucking good at this business, Paddy lad, I thought. Company car, travel expenses and such friendly customers. My main target market was taxi drivers. I would pull up beside them at traffic lights. 'Hey, driver. Had many tips today? Well, I have the tip of the century for you, bud. PFF, Paddy for Fuel. Have a glorious day now, salutations, fellow knight of the road.'

I was, however, in no time at all, running out of petrol stations locally, and therefore I was forced to expand my empire further afield, to the point where I started hitting the motorway service stations. Now these were easier, due to the hustle and bustle and commotion. The problem I was facing was that they were sort of out of my way. I was losing free money. Plus, the mileage on my hire was pushing it towards an oil change. Who would I send the invoice to for that? It's tough running your own empire, people.

So, I got a little bit cheeky. I would pull up at the pump as usual. Top up my expenses first. Then I would begin to fill my empties. Once the pump cut out, I would then head to the cashier and say, 'Excuse me. I am in the process of filling up a type-approved diesel storage tank in my boot over there. It's actually fuels for one of the small fleet of pleasure craft that I operate on the canals. The pump, however, has cut out at one hundred pounds.'

'Okay, sir. No problem. Just let me reset that for you.' And they did.

'Thank you ever so kindly.'

I was making a steady mint out of this for a few weeks. I knew it wasn't going to last long. Unless I changed car and grew a beard. It got me out of the house too during the days.

I was still taking my little baby girl to and from school every day. The school was only ten to fifteen minutes' walk from where we lived. I would stand in the playground, amongst the mere mortals. Fucking cattle, the lot of them. Do-gooding bastards, all of them, I would think. Then the doors would open and the litter would run out. I would spot my little angel in amongst the rush. Little red cardigan, white polo shirt buttoned all the way to the top, covering her tiny neck. Little pleated black skirt with black tights. Hair up in two little pigtails. She would see me and come running over, all excited, holding a picture or a drawing. 'Wuk, Dadth.' She had a little lisp as a baby. 'Wuk what I dwared, iths goodth, isn't it, Dadth?' Her little face all happy, looking up to me. We would walk back to our house holding hands. Her little tiny hand in mine. Talking about her teachers and who she was playing with in school and what she had eaten for her dinner.

That is surely enough for any fucking man, isn't it? If you fucking call yourself a man. That's enough to slam your fucking two feet on that brake and give your best to this little girl who deserves, fucking you. Her dad. Now, I hate myself for this, I really fucking do. It just wasn't in my diagram at that time. I am so sorry, my baby girl. I love you so much.

It was one of those days. I was due to pick up my baby from school at three thirty. (Half three, kids. Big hand on six and the little hand on three.) I had overcooked my timings whilst out on manoeuvres and was running a bit late. I was driving like a mad man to try and get back on time for the school. I did make it on time. However, I had also, in the melee, cut up and allegedly verbally abused an off-duty police officer, who had then instantly reported the incident, together with the car details to the powers that be. The fucking grass.

A couple of nights after this, whilst back out on manoeuvres, I reversed into an alleyway, near to my home. My intentions were to have a cheeky couple of fat lines of vit C before I went home. I didn't want Emma thinking that I was on drugs. Fucking dickhead Paddy when I look back. Every fucking one knew. Even the dog. Anyway. I racked up a couple of big fat lines of vit C on a CD case. Rolled up a ten-pound tent, stuck it up a nostril. Then shoulders back, head down. I was just about to begin nasal suction when, tap-tap at the driver's window.

The CD went flying out of my hands as I jumped. Fuck me, what was that? I turned and looked at my window. Who was standing there? The fucking police. And who was staring at them? Me, with a rolled up note hanging out of his nostril. I was well and truly fucking nicked. The worst of it was, these fuckers were on push bikes. Paddy, I thought. You are in a fucking car, you tit. How can you get nicked by the cycle plod? The car, my fucking car, I found out shortly afterwards, had been reported by the grass earlier and was subsequently tied in with evidence, showing clear CCTV images of me and the vehicle at various petrol stations, looking all sexy and handsome stealing fuel.

Back then, stealing fuel wasn't a crime as such. It wasn't a charge. It was bracketed as a domestic incident for some reason. It was only after that, that it became a criminal offence. Theft of fuel, or bilking, to give it its charge offence title. Now, I am not saying that the law was changed because of me. However, if it was, then surely, I should have been given the honour of naming that law. I wouldn't have called it bilking. I would have called it milking. Clever bastard, me, eh? Or is that just a dad joke where only I laugh? I can't fucking tell these days.

I will tell you one thing though about getting older. The fucking shocks your body puts your poor brain through are fucking ruthless, aren't they? I always check my bollocks when

I am in the bath. I don't mean check them out, like, yeah, look at them bad boys. I mean medically, for anomalies, lumps, etcetera. I would urge all men to do it to be fair.

Anyway, a few weeks ago, I was in the bath. Candlelight all around me. Barry White doing his thing on my MP3. I gave it the old check. I slapped my ball sack onto my thigh. Like the man dropping off a sack of coal. Right, Paddy, let's have a fumble with these here spuds. Give them the onceover. Fuck me. There. Right in front my eyes. Laid across my ball sack like a comb over, trying to blend into the background, acting all innocent and casual. A fucking grey pubic hair. Well, fuck me.

My temperature went through the bastard roof. The water was bubbling. Where the fuck did that creep in from? You have got to go, mate. All of my other pubes started clapping and shouting, 'Out, out, out, out.' I pulled it, but it wouldn't budge. Every time I yanked it, my arsehole would tense up.

I could hear my arsehole shouting upstairs to my brain, 'Paddy, Paddy. Who the fuck's that, eh? No one ever knocks here, Paddy lad. I am a bit worried, Paddy, I'm all alone down here.'

I had to cut it out in the end with scissors, which made my balls wince. 'Ohhhhh, fucking careful, Paddy mate, you're sailing a bit close to the wind there, Paddy. Slow and steady wins the race, Paddy, sloww and steady, Paddy.'

Anyway, back on track. So, I am unfairly arrested and treated like a criminal. The car, my fucking car, is taken away to be impounded for the ascertainers to ascertain shit. Lovely fucking car by the way, Mr Enterprise. Quite nippy and really good on fuel. Very economical. I was taken to a police station at a place called Skemesdale, on the outskirts of Liverpool. It's a town basically made out of roundabouts. I was taken there because of the footage and reports and probably the grass were all from that area.

I was held overnight in custody, interviewed the following

morning and then dropped off back at my home by a police officer. Actually, one of the few sound ones to be fair. When I got home, poor Emma was in despair. Beside herself. 'Paddy. Where the fuck have you been? I have been worried sick.'

'Chill the fuck out, Emma love, for fuck's sake. I have just been let out, haven't I?' As if I had just been released from a ten stretch. 'I got fucking nicked last night, didn't I?'

'What for, Paddy? Why are you doing this to us?'

'Fucking hell, Emma, give me a break. I was caught crossing a fucking zebra crossing sideways. All right?' What a cocky, horrible bastard I was then. You know, if there were such a thing as a time machine, I wouldn't do the old, let's go back in time and get the euro millions numbers. I would go back to then. That moment. I would run into that house and batter the fucking living shite out of myself. Then do a few star jumps just to freak Emma out, then run up the stairs, slide back down on my arse, get up and moonwalk out of the door. Then gone. No, you must have been dreaming, Emma love; he did what?

I did however tell my dad. I had to. He was one of my gold customers. 'I've gone bankrupt, Dad. The business has folded. Supply issues.' My dad took me up to the police station in his black cab a couple of weeks later, where I was given an official caution, by the same officer who dropped me home actually. The caution was for possession of cocaine and something else relating to the fuel. I can't really remember the exact term. I never did find out what happened to that ten pound note that was up my nostril. Maybe it's still up there. I will have to check. Or maybe the police took it, and that's why they dropped me home that day. Because I had chipped in for petrol.

CHAPTER 15
A low blow even for me

Now, this chapter is a bit cringeworthy for me, and embarrassing. But it's essential to this book and the truth. Now, before you judge me after reading this, that's if you haven't already, I please urge you to take a closer look at yourself. I apologise if that sounds rude. It is not intended to. It's because, as aforementioned, this book is about the truth. My family and loved ones deserve the truth. It is the least that I can do for all the pain and heartache that I have caused over the years. Paddy the walking question mark. The enigma that I became. I can't work Patrick out. Well, after you finish this book, you should have all of answer that you need.

Everybody has something that they are ashamed of. Everybody. I don't care who you are. The majority of you will take that to the grave with you. Mine is going out there. I have the balls to stick mine out in the public domain. Why? Because it's all about the truth, people. It's fessing up time. Absolve one's sins. I am not part of the God Squad. I am not trying to preach. I am a Christian, and I do believe in our Lord. The end. As I say, just look historically at your own past, back to a certain time and place, before judging me.

So here I was. On cloud ten, moving onto eleven. I was not keeping up with my sustenance, eating and drinking properly, like any normal person. I was mixing my drugs up. All sorts of drugs. I had them hidden all over the house. Always out of reach of my baby girl, but. But they were everywhere. It was like a game of *Hungry Hippos* with me at times. I would just search around my house, my stash points. Yom, gulp, snort. Next. I was losing weight to the point where, one night, one of the rare nights I would actually go to bed, I was getting undressed, unclipping the shoulder strap that held my cock in place. Then suddenly Emma just stared at me, mouth wide open in shock.

'Paddy. Oh my God. Why the fuck are you wearing my knickers?' 'Paddy. Oh my God. How much weight have you lost?' I remember that moment very well for some reason. I had subconsciously been wearing extra layers of clothes to hide the fact that I was losing weight. My clothes were basically hanging off me. I looked into the mirror. (I do that a lot these days. I get better-looking every day. I can't wait until tomorrow.)

'Oh fucking hell, Emma. Finally, I can fit into your little black dress. I bet you're well jel, aren't you? I am sooo exited. I am going to get my nails done tomorrow. My eyeballs waxed. Not eyeballs, eyebrows, I meant. That would fucking hurt that, wouldn't it? Getting your fucking eyeballs waxed. I am going to get a full facial and a spray tan. Then I can be orange. Just like all the other girls in Liverpool. Fucking Umpa Lumpas in pyjamas taking their kids to school.'

I looked into that mirror. Paddy, I said to myself. Take a fucking good hard look at yourself. What's happening to you? I felt vulnerable at that point. Almost as if Emma were bullying me. So, I just stared into that mirror and sang, 'You are beautiful, no matter what they say. Words can't bring me down. Owe no no noo noo, coz you rrr beautiful… I didn't know what I thought at that point to be honest. Anyway, Paddy. Easily solved, this, with a couple of thick jumpers and a coat. Won't look odd at all this summer. It will take the attention off your eyeballs anyway.

Emma's dad. Rob. Another legend of a bloke. He was always

joking about, taking the piss out of people. He loved his wife and his kids dearly and cherished his grandkids. Not a bad bone in the guy's body. He had unfortunately taken ill. So, it was all hands to the pump type of thing with the family. Everybody was taking it in turns as a family, ensuring that he wasn't alone in the hospital. Trying to balance their working lives and family commitments, etcetera, to make this work.

Emma's family, like my own family, are hardworking and decent, honest people. However, like mine, they also don't suffer fools. Fuck it up and you will know about it. Whatever it takes. That old saying. If the finger turns green with gangrene, you chop it off to save the hand. That saying springs to mind. I was becoming that finger. I don't know why I was turning green. It must have had something to do with me cutting about with all the aliens on my regular visits to the moon.

It was later that afternoon that I found a piece of wood sticking out of Emma's handbag. Now, I never usually went into Emma's bag; she never had any fucking money in it anyway. Banker's people. Fucking coy as fuck, they are. Unless it was to borrow some moisturiser or foundation, a bit of lip gloss, that sort of thing. Anyway, I pulled out this bit of wood. Fuck me, it's an axe. She is going to cut me up. I must explain the meaning of that phrase to her before it's too late. I was becoming a burden. A green finger. I, her man, was mentally fucking draining her.

Her family were aware of this. Her poor dad, Rob, was in hospital fighting for his life. I should have been there for her. The strong arm. Reassuring her and comforting her. Holding her together to the best of my ability with the support she needed and the understating of the requirement to adapt to such a situation. Me, however, and my blinkered views on the situation thought that doing such things as transporting family to and from the hospital and shopping and all the easy stuff was enough.

I guess I may have subconsciously thought that if I was involved in this way, my way, I might just stay that bit more emotionally detached from the whole situation, thus making life easier for me. Like one of those lazy bastards, when you are tasked to do a job or an operation as a group, and you always get one fat fucking lazy fucktard that picks out the easiest part of that operation for themselves. Non-game players. I fucking terrorise people like that on my boat these days. I play a game to myself that I created. Spot the cunt. 'Right, you fucking fat lazy cunt. Follow me. I have a different job for you.'

Anyway. That was my idea at that time of being there for her. Basically, a useless and uncaring bastard. Now, prior to Rob taking ill, I had run a few errands for him. He would give me his cash card, and I would then go shopping for him to get him what he needed. Once finished, I would give him the shopping, together with his card, change and receipts. Now, that was normal, right? Well now, poor Rob was in hospital in a really bad way. The family was falling apart. I couldn't go out on my manoeuvres because I had my baby Amy to look after, more than usual. Plus, I was ferrying family up and down to the hospital, picking up people from work. All the hard stuff. This is so unfair on you, Paddy. I hope they are all appreciating this. Of course, they were. But it wasn't about me. However, I needed my drugs. I couldn't get out to do my thing, so I therefore had very little finance. The cunt within was already making his demands, threatening me.

'Paddeeyyyyyyyyyyyy.' Sniff sniff. 'We must act now. We are on the brink of war.' Sniff sniff. 'The mere mortals are pushing forward, Paddeeyyyyyyyyyyyy. They are threatening to overthrow us.' Sniff sniff. What the fuck do you want me to do about it cunt, eh? My hands are well and truly tied up here. I can't back you up, cunt, I just can't. It's impossible.

'Paddeeyyyyyyyyyyyyy.' Sniff sniff. 'What has four numbers and sounds like "Fin"? But unlike a fish, it's your number one wish.' Fuck off, cunt, you twat. I haven't got time for fucking *Scrabble*, or *Guess Who*, or whatever the fuck it is you want me to play. 'PIN, Paddeeyyyyyyyyyyyyy. PIN, PIN, PIN, PIN, PIN. Now I must rest. SLEEP, SLEEP, SLEEP, SLEEP, SLEEP.' Oi. Fucking wake up, scumbag. Oi, CUNT, wake up. Nothing. It's gone. That horrid little creature. What does it mean? Pin?

Oh, I know what it meant. Pin. Rob's pin number for his bank card. Fuck me, cunt. Just when I thought you couldn't get any lower. I knew where Rob's bank card was kept in his house. And I had keys. So, I started to help myself whilst the poor guy was in hospital and the family was distraught. I know. What a guy I am, eh? It was always with the intention of replacing the cash before anybody found out. It wasn't stealing at that time in my eyes. It was more of an essential loan to keep me drugged up and focused so that I could continue my ferrying and shopping of course.

Now, in my eyes it seemed as if everybody, outside of the Emma, Amy and Paddy bubble, was of the opinion that Paddy was making a real effort here. But an observer sees more of the game, right? He is not out, gallivanting around doing his own thing as per usual. I actually overheard a conversation between Emma and her lovely sister, Dawn. They were praising me, I think.

It reached a point in the end. It was way fucking out of control, this. I just couldn't pay it back. Everybody, including mates, knew that I was on a different planet and therefore closed all financial support. It's okay, Paddy I would think. Just don't be worrying. Cunt will get us out of this. It always does. Then, it hit crucial. Oh fucking fuck. Rob was getting discharged from hospital in a couple of days. Fantastic news obviously, but my arse was now twitching like a rabbit's nose. What was I going to do?

So, with all avenues blocked off and doors closed, cunt and I jumped into the car and just fucked off. Like fucking Thelma and Louise. I had left poor, distraught Emma a note explaining what I had done and told her that I wouldn't be returning. What a fucking cunt's trick, eh? A coward's way out. I couldn't face the shame.

I had been on the missing list for a few days. I was out of town. I didn't actually get too far to be fair. I just sort of skimmed the outskirts. Just me, the cunt and a carload of drugs. I was trying to get an hour's sleep in a car park one particular night. I only needed a couple of hours to reset certain brain cells, delete a few cookies. Sleep deficit had caught up me big time. I was seeing double, together with the odd hallucination. My brain was just yearning to sleep, and therefore it was, albeit it with my eyes open. Sort of like shutting down a valuable, critical piece of equipment, whereby you need to hold the button in, and the machine counts down from ten to zero. You release the button at zero and the machine shuts down.

My machine was counting down on the button, sleeping until I wobbled my head and released that button. Then I was awake again. It was getting towards zero rapidly though. The problem was, I couldn't sleep. Apart from being wired to the moon, I was sitting upright. The driver's seat was broken. I had tried to adapt it by doing something daft, like installing an electric wheelchair motor to its mechanical gibbons. Obviously, that didn't work, and so I had tried to repair the driver's seat with parts from the passenger seat. However, I had fucked that one up too. So, I was essentially sitting bolt upright with the posture of a fucking set square. I was like one of those miniature Spitfire pilots on an Airfix model.

Suddenly, a car enters this pitch-black car park. Now, I am the only other car in this car park. It stops right at the back of me, its headlights on full beam. Blinding me. That's not a car, Paddy, it's a fucking UFO. They have come for you because the last time you were on the moon you stole five hundred zonks from the post office up there. I thought, shit, that's the police. I grabbed all my drugs slowly and shoved them down my pants next to my balls, the cock shouting up to my brain, 'Waheyyyy, it's party time, whoop whoop.' Shut the fuck up, cock. We have a situation here.

The car just stayed there for fucking time, just blinding the shite out of me. Next thing, tap, tap, tap on my window, torch in my face. I didn't even see him coming in all the light. Now he has a torch in my face. What is it with these cunts and fucking light bulbs? I opened my door. The police dude in front of me was just a fucking blur, but I could smell the bacon. 'Sir, could you please come and join us in the back of our car?' Why are we all getting in the back of his car, I thought That's a bit gay.

I got into the back of the unmarked police car. Actually, looking back, it looked dodgy as fuck. Two cars in a deserted dark car park. His car lit up like a hillbilly's pickup truck chasing a kangaroo. If a police patrol car comes into the car park, they think a drug deal is going down. Imagine that, plain-clothed police and the fucking Robocops battling it out in the car park. The battle of the bastards. These officers were, however, very sympathetic and very understanding and kind to my situation. You see, engage people, like humans, with your hearts in it, like a person, not like fucking Metal Micky (Google it, kids), and you

112

will get more in return and appreciate your job a little better.

The stigma you have is a combination of both your own failings plus the public's wrongdoing. Work on your own failings first with proper management, and slowly the second factor will start pulling away. Connect your tasers to your testicles, rigged up to a Cuntometer, and every time you speak to people like a cunt, you receive a shock to the balls. Of course, you will have to carry a whole range of spare batteries with you. I can't sort out the logistical side of it though, boys, that's down to you.

Anyway. The reason they had investigated my presence in the car park was because I had been reported as missing, and my car matched the descriptions, etcetera. That was one reason. The other was obviously because I looked a bit suspect and sort of stood out, alone in an empty car park. They are really clever, these police, you know. It's not all burgers, bullying and driving like fucking pricks.

This continued for a few days. I was changing my clothes at motorway service stations and washing my body with a sponge. I would fill up the sink with water and lob my cock and bollocks into it whilst having a shave. I would watch them floating about in the water, the bollocks taking it in turns sliding off the cock and into the water below. Ahhhh, look at the two of them, I would think. It's not their fault, any of this, either. They don't deserve this. 'Wheeeeeee,' they would shout, all excited. Right, c'mon now, boys. Out the pool, get dried off and back in the barracks. 'Rrrr. Just five more minutes,' they would plead, 'pleaseee pleaseeee.' No. C'mon, boys, back in the underpants now. There is a queue of confused-looking cattle behind me here, waiting to wash their hands.

It got to the point whereby I had had enough. I wanted to go home. I had had enough. I was still on a different planet, but enough was enough. I wanted to go home and lay down. Surely they would have forgiven me by now? They were all probably sitting there now. All huddled around the telephone. Just waiting for it to ring. I was half-expecting one of those planes with a banner hanging out of its arse to fly over with, 'PLEASE COME HOME, PADDY. WE NEED YOU' wafting in the wind.

I found a telephone box (a sort of rectangle thing, kids, with, guess what? A phone inside). I phoned Emma, punching myself a few times in the throat first to give that wounded sort of impression. 'Emma.' Cough, cough. 'It's me. Paddy.' Silence. 'Emma. It's me.' Cough, cough, cough. For fuck's sake, Emma, I was thinking. Hurry up. I've only got twenty pence left.

'Paddy. Just come home,' she said.

'Okay, I will. But, but, but, but I am so sorry, Emma.'

'Just come home, Paddy.' The line went dead. I slowly placed down the telephone receiver (Google Images, kids) and slowly opened the telephone box door.

'Fucking result!' I shouted. I started skipping back over to my car, stopping to allow a cat to pass in front of me. 'No, after you, sir, I insist. Aren't you a lovely little scabby-looking thing?' The cat gave me one of those, you're a weird bastard sort of looks. Into the car. A splash of Brut 33 on the face. You might even get to play out tonight, cock. I started up the engine. Now all aboard, people. Next stop. Home.

I didn't know, or didn't register, all of the heartache that I had caused at this point. The impact of my actions upon everybody else. The heartache and worry I had put people through with my own selfish actions. The switchboard, people. If yours is broken, if it starts to develop issues, get it fixed. Family are the answer. They are the technicians. The ones with the diagnostic equipment. They can install that software to your hardware and fix you. But you must be you for this process to take place. The drugs, and/or drink must go. It's hard, I know, but also achievable, and the rewards are amazing. Once it's gone, it's gone forever.

So, I then pulled into my road. I could see from a distance that there were a lot of people outside my house. Right, okay, Paddy. It's obviously a welcome home committee for you. As I got closer, I could see my dad's black cab parked outside. I got a bit closer. Okay, Paddy, I can't see any balloons yet. There is nobody clapping and waving either, jumping up and down with joy. Something really odd about this, Paddy.

I pulled up outside my home. My dad came straight over to me. 'Son. Give me the car keys.' So I did. 'Now, get in the back of the cab with your mother, son.' I was just staring at Emma, searching for an answer to what was happening. Why, Emma? The look on her face said it all. My mum came over to me and walked me over to my dad's cab. She opened the door and I climbed in the back. There were a couple of big bags laid out on the floor in the cab. 'What's that, Mum?'

'It's your belongings, son. You're coming home with us. You can't stay in that house any more.' I watched my dad hand Emma the car keys and then give her a hug. He then climbed into the cab and we drove away. I was searching the group outside for my little angel. Where was she? Where was my baby girl? She wasn't there. Emma had removed her from that situation. Shielded her. Protected her from the pain. She always has, and I thank her with all of my heart for that. An amazing mother, you have been, and more importantly, continue to be, Emma.

Thank you, Emma. To all of Emma's family. I deeply apologise for putting you all through that ordeal. To my own mum and dad. Thanks again. You have always been there to catch me.

CHAPTER 16
The comeback

So, now I was back living with the parents plus my two younger brothers, Paul and Francis, both lovely and honest hardworking lads. Reality started hitting me big time. The drug's effects had worn off. I had to. I fucking had to get my two girls back. We were a unit. The three of us. I would do whatever it took to get them back. However, these fucking clouds, a selection of horrible black clouds, evil-looking bastards, were just engulfing the inside of my head. They were all holding their own emotional, poisonous precipitation, releasing the downpour as and when they wanted. All bumping into each other, confused. Sending me into states of mania.

So, into the rooms comes Gandalf, without the big stick and the daft beard. Or my dad as I call him. The white-haired wizard. 'You need to get yourself fit, son. You need to start training. Don't be thinking about your home or work, because none of that is going to happen just yet. Get yourself fit.' He handed me an old grey tracksuit with holes all over it and a pint glass with a dozen eggs.

'Set your alarm clock for three a.m. Get up, open the fridge. Crack the eggs into the glass, then go out jogging around town. Keep up this routine until a crowd of kids start to run behind you shouting, Paddy, Paddy. When the moment is right, just sprint and leave the little bastards for dust. Find a load of stairs and run up them as fast as you can, being careful not to trip over. When you reach the top, jump up and down as if you have just knocked out your first wank. Then, son. You are ready. Eye of the moggy, son. Eye of the moggy.'

I did. I cut all drugs and drink out of my life. Not even a fucking wine gum. I started weight training and circuit training during the days. Then of an evening I would go out jogging with my brothers, a bit of sparring in the back yard. My system and mind cleared out. Zero toxins. I was eating properly, thanks to my mum and training both alone, and with my brothers, of whom one turned out to be a talented kickboxer and the other a talented boxer.

The clouds were beginning to stabilise. Then, one by one, they were rubbed out. Erased. I still had my sad moments of course, but these moments were becoming a lot more manageable as I began to process and understand them more. The latter can only be achieved whilst drug and drink free. You simply cannot have the both. Route A or B. Route A is full of rewards. Route B is full of regrets. It's that simple. The end.

I still wasn't ready to go back to sea though. Don't get me wrong, I love the sea, I really do, but apart from all the good times and memories I had, I still had sad ones. So best leave that there for now, Paddy, until I am a bit stronger. So, I found a job in a factory. The job was making the inner linings and fitting them to the insides of spectacle cases and jewellery boxes. The hours, as I remember, were eight a.m. to 5 p.m.

This was in early 2000-ish, when back then the common language spoken in such factories wasn't Polish or Russian or Bulgarian. It was English. It was okay, a good little steady job. It was routine, and it was what I needed for harmonising and enhancing my life's path. I would wake in the morning, feeling nice and refreshed after a solid, sober night's sleep. I would have my breakfast, then into my car and off to work. How normal can you get? I would then come home, back to my parents. Have my dinner prepared by my mum. Then an hour's chilling, then I would weight train and then out jogging. The money was shite compared to what I made at sea. Not even a fraction of what I was used to. However, relative to my outgoings without the drugs in my life, it was okay. I would take out my expenses for fuel and my lunches and give the rest to Emma and Amy. My mum didn't want any housekeeping. She just wanted me to do the right thing.

It was fucking awesome. It was going great. Lovely in fact. Emma was starting to invite me around to the house for my dinner. We would all eat together, the three of us, then watch a movie or a bit of TV together. I would then go back home to my parents. It was enough, at that time anyway. The way it should be. Nobody was being overwhelmed. It was nice and steady, consensual. Her family were very supporting of this, apart from her sister, Dawn. She had seen all of this as an attack on her family. Like I had betrayed her and them. I had in a way, and I totally understand that now. Dynamics again, people.

I know that I have mentioned this word a lot so far, but it is the key to our being, our individuality. Even in my profession. We have such things as sister ships. Two ships built identically, using the same schematics, layouts, steel, hardware and systems. Aesthetically they are identical: every angle, every frame looks the same part for part. However, any mariner that knows his game will tell you that they are completely different. They act differently under different conditions. They do not handle the same; they give you feedback in different ways. I suppose identical aircraft would act the same? I don't know this for a fact as I am not a pilot, although I've flown quite a few space missions. A friend of mine and my daughter Amy is though. Captain Jock Hamilton. A fucking legend of a bloke. Both a

Master Mariner and a 747 aircraft pilot and also an ex- Royal Marine Commando.

What I am trying to get at is, our minds are our own, right? They cannot be cloned. Shit affects the individual on a different level, right? Such as Dawn, Emma's sister. We all react to shit differently. So, how then, if that's the case, can the treatment be the same? It can't be, can it? It doesn't add up to me. I am not saying that treatment doesn't work. But you have to back it up with your own defences. I am off tangent here a bit. I am referring to drug-induced and many bogus mental states and causes and certain treatments.

I know a lot of you at this point will think, hang on, Paddy. There is a process for the above. First, you see a psychoanalyst, who will determine what is wrong with you, and then a psychotherapist for the treatment. Yes, I am well aware of this. I have been there many a time. However, back the fuck up. I know what is wrong with me. I have a drug issue. So why have I been sent here? Why has the buck been passed? Do you honestly believe I was born with eyeballs like this?

Mother Nature herself was at a picnic on the day that they made me. It was a late Friday afternoon. She had drunk a bit too much holy water and was wiped out. She wanted to knock off early. 'Excuse me, Mother Nature. We are just in the process of creating this boy child here. We seem to have run out of eyeballs though. Angel direct parcel services cannot deliver until Monday. What are we to do?'

'I know,' says Mother Nature. 'Take a couple of those white saucers out of my picnic basket. Slot them into the eye sockets. A dab of blue paint with a black dot in the middle. Throw in one of those extra-large cocks just to sweeten the deal. Job's a goodun. See you Monday.'

It's fucking obvious I have an underlying and obvious issue, you fucking bell end. So I don't need you sitting there, all fucking smug, legs crossed with a notebook and pen in your hand. In a room where I can only hear a ticking clock. You are stereotyping yourself before we begin, being that slave to convention. I knew what to expect as soon as I entered the room. I could picture it, and there is that mental image, it's you. In this fucking silent room, legs crossed in a leather chair, holding a pen and a fucking notebook and wearing glasses, even though you have probably got fifty-fifty vision. Why? I will fucking tell you why. Because your book says you must do this. The rule book of the psyche. Another fucking textbook that you are afraid to deviate from.

'Try to relax, Patrick'. Don't fucking tell me to relax. And don't call me Patrick. There are two things you should have already addressed before we started this bullshit. What I like and don't like. And what I like to be named. Instead, you assume from your textbook that this is acceptable. To tell a stranger to relax and speak to them as if you know them. Tailor this fucking experience to my needs. My desires. Put some music on in the background and make it a space I can relax in. I am paying for the privilege of being undermined by a fucking twenty-four-year-old life-inexperienced prick.

Put down the pen and paper. You are only playing fucking Sudoku anyway, killing time. I didn't have a bad upbringing. Nobody came into my bedroom as a child and did the unimaginable to me. I was bought up, I wasn't dragged up. There was no reason for me to turn to drugs in the first place, other than I wanted to. It was my choice. I am sorry for being a bit over the top here, people. It just makes my fucking shit itch, how we approach issues with this cotton wool, political bullshit.

A fucking nonce (not of normal criminal element) sex

offender, a predatory fucking sick scumbag can offload his or her emotions to these people and receive treatment. Fuck you. One cure. Chop of the fucking cock and stitch it to their heads. Believe me, the trend would soon stop. There are plenty of dickheads cutting about on our planet but not many with an actual cock on their heads.

This is not drugged up Paddy the ignorant speaking here. That prick is well and truly out of the door. This is Paddy the father. Paddy the carer. Paddy the realist. You can't say these things any more, Paddy, it's not allowed in today's world. Well, you can keep today's world, its shit and soft. I prefer the earlier, more tough and real one. How will this stop that trend, Paddy? Through consequence analysis of course. You know that you are going to lose your cock and have it stitched to your head, so you therefore want to manage that risk. You will know the consequences if you fuck it. You don't need a psychoanalyst for that, you dirty bastard. You just need to understand the risk. Your brain will process that risk naturally and install the necessary hardware into your switchboard.

Then we have treatment. The psychotherapy. acupuncture and fucking whale music? Why are you sticking pins in my ears and making me listen to a fish? If that was on a Tinder profile, I like to listen to fish whilst dressing up a fucking porcupine, you would swipe right, wouldn't you? A fucking weird one, that one. I am not discounting acupuncture as treatment by the way, people, as it is medically proven to help. But not me. My brain is more of a sort of, what the fuck's this nonsense, Paddy, type of thing.

Now, I know that you eagle-eyed intellects will at this point be saying to yourselves, you are contradicting yourself here, Paddy. Earlier you said that risk and consequence analyses were natural processes that you adapt to and understand over time. Yes, I did. But that's not my point here. If we can use the following analogy as an example. There is a subtle difference between losing, let's say, a loved one and losing your cock, right? Losing a partner at some stage in your life, whether it is through infidelity or boredom or whatever, is a part of life that a huge amount of the world's population will suffer. Now, this risk for the latter is medium and the severity is harmful. That alone in a lot of people is not enough for their switchboard to prioritise the consequence on the correct scale. That's why people have affairs and such things.

Now, if you commit a severe sex crime, for example, and ruin your poor victim's existence, and if the punishment for committing such a horrid crime was a mandatory cock on the block, then that risk is very high and the severity is off the fucking scale. Your switchboard would immediately prioritise that consequence and you would keep your cock.

My conclusion: if I had been told, right, Paddy, give up the drugs or your cock's on the block, I would have instantly given up. The end. Flip that coin over. Paddy, give up the drugs or you will lose the woman you love together with your identity as a family man. I wouldn't and evidently didn't.

Therefore, we all have the power to do this. Whether it's naturally by means of our switchboards adapting over time or our switchboards are force-fed the data necessary to shock and/or enhance that risk and prioritise the management of that risk accordingly. If we learn to manage our risks through understanding them, we have saved ourselves major ball ache. The latter is not a reference to mental health. That is totally different. The unbalanced and rather painful levels of depression versus individual and brain functions, which do exist commonly, are not to be taken lightly. As aforementioned, the latter was aimed at drug use and scumbags who use life traumas, etcetera, as a rite of passage to commit atrocities.

Things for me and my little family, the Fambo, continued to carry on in this way for a good time. As sweet as a fucking nut. Family life. There is no substitute. Being a man. Loving your family. Providing for them and protecting them. Making them laugh and feel happy. It's the perfect world.

Emma started letting me stay over on the occasional night. We would put on our matching pyjamas, make a tent in the living room out of blankets and eat loads of ice cream and tell ghost stories. Then we would hear noises outside the house and scream then run upstairs to wake Amy up. 'Amy, we are scared, can we please get in bed with you?' Again, it was nice and slow. We had the rest of our lives together. What was the rush?

We would do date nights. I would play the woman and she would play the man. She wouldn't shave her legs for days, just to get into character. She really went all out, did Emma. I wouldn't drink on our date nights. Neither did Emma. Not because I had asked her not to, but because she didn't want to. Again she wanted this to work. Wanted me to be mended. She was supporting me by silently and commendably covering all she could at her end. It was either that or she was worried that when asleep I would be hovering over her face, trying to sniff the booze, like Hannibal Lecter. Licking her lips like a creepy fucker as she slept. Eventually I moved back into the house. I had a lot of work to do and a lot of bridges to mend.

We bought Amy a pair of dwarf rabbits from some breeder guy. They were lovely little things, they were. Lilo and Stitch, Amy called them. We had a rabbit hutch in the garden, and I built an extension enclosing the hutch. A sort of run, if you like. Caged in with chicken wire. Like a prison exercise yard. Like a prison to be fair, albeit with a better selection of food and without the gang rape. It kept the rabbits safe from cats and other predators.

The problem was, as per their title, dwarf rabbits, these things were fucking tiny. Even though I had doubled up on the cross formation on the chicken wire, these little fuckers were still escaping. Not together, like Bonny and Clyde (that would have been a more appropriate name, Amy); these things would make a run for it alone. I would often go to check on them.

'Oh fuck, Emma. Another one's bolted.'

Then, at some point shortly afterwards, a neighbour would knock at our house. KNOCK, KNOCK. That's how they knocked. 'I am sorry to tell you this, but I think one of Amy's rabbits is dead in our garden.' The poor little fuckers didn't get too far without being savaged by an alley cat or similar. I would then have to go to my new dealer before Amy found out. The fucking rabbit dealer (I know) didn't turn out to be all nice and fluffy.

'Eh, mate,' I would say. 'I don't suppose you have any of those dwarf rabbits left, have you?'

'What are you doing with these things? You're not eating them, are you?' What a fucking question.

'No, mate. I am making bunny teddies. The kids love them.' Eating them. The fucking dickhead. In the end he ran out of them. 'Shit, Emma. What are we going to do? What if I buy a normal-sized rabbit, paint it grey and then stick it in a vice?' Imagine that. A tiny compressed rabbit; it would just be a massive pair of fluffy eyeballs, wouldn't it? It would look a bit like me on speed.

Eh, I seen Paddy the other day. He looks like he has been twatted in the eye sockets by a pair of matching golf balls. The poor bastard was playing in the cemetery on a pogo stick. Singing that annoying twat Timmy Mallet's song. 'She wore an itsy bitsy teeny weeny yellow polka dot bikini, that she wore for the first time today. OH YEAH.' He is one mad bastard, that feller. My poor little baby girl Amy couldn't understand why her rabbits looked all confused when she picked them up, like, who the fuck are you type of look.

'Dadth, my wabbiths wooks sadt.' First encounter, sorry, baby girl. Just didn't have the heart to tell her. Although now she knows. They all went to rabbit heaven, love. Every time it thunders, that's them bouncing on the clouds. Honest.

So, here is Paddy living the dream. A beautiful, intelligent and funny, shit cook of a fiancée and an equally all-rounder daughter. Although Amy can cook, she really can. She cooked me a meal at my apartment a few weeks ago. Fucking awesome, it was. Although she used every fucking pan and pot in the kitchen and left me the mess. The scruffy little shit. I haven't really researched what the difference is between a pan and a pot. One of life's unanswered questions, eh? I've often wondered too. Let's say if a cow was born in a field full of dogs. Would it grow up mooing or barking? There're no fucking mirrors in a field, right? How does it know it's not a dog? Another one of those head fuck questions same time tomorrow, people.

Although I had all of the above, it wasn't enough for my family. My two girls deserved more. Truth be told, due to my fuck ups, I had got us into a bit of debt. We could have easily managed as we were. We were not going to go hungry, put it that way. And we could pay the bills and manage the debt. But it wasn't enough. I am the man. I must give my family the life that they are used to. That life that these two deserve.

I had always earned good, honest money before all of this. We always had disposable income. Even with the drug binges.

With my one month on, one month off rotations and of course Emma's salary, the cash was always there for holidays, days out, anything. Emma wasn't bothered one bit about this, looking back, bless her. She was just happy that I had returned from my space mission and we were all happy again as a family. Paddy Mark One. The real man.

Nope. It's just not enough, Paddy lad. You must take that club, face that saber-toothed tiger, smash its fucking head in and drag it back into the cave and feed your family. Although let Amy or yourself cook it. Emma can just peel the spuds; she can't really fuck that up, and she will feel included. Just pat her on the head in a non-patronising sort of way. 'Well done, Emma, really nice curves on them there spuds, love. They will taste delicious.' I wasn't ready to go back on a boat. I just didn't feel as though I could mentally take the pain.

So, I cracked open that Yellow Pages again. (Yep, kids, that one again. Similar shape, if not identical shape to a phone box. Rectangle.) I searched local companies for ideas. Bingo. 'Emma, lend me twenty fucking pence. I have got to make a phone call.' I liked the sound of this.

CHAPTER 17
Mr Whippy

The job I had decided to go for was working as an ice cream man. I know. As if I wasn't delicious enough. It was just something that appealed to me at that time. It was nice, innocent and fresh. I had a nice, colourful van with Disney characters stencilled onto it. I was out and about, chatting with little kids. I like kids (to a degree). I like the innocence and truth you get from a child. Although, after a few weeks, they were starting to annoy me. They would all gather around my ice cream van, like fucking leaches. 'Can I please have, erm, erm, erm, erm, a Funny Foot? No, sorry, can I pleasssseeee have an erm, erm, erm, what can I get for nine pence?' For fuck's sake.

'There's a Flump. Now piss off. Next.' I would take Amy with me sometimes at the weekends. There was no passenger seating in the van, so I would just plonk her in the sink on a cushion next to me. It was her job to hit the tune switch, which played Popeye, funnily enough. Bizarre, eh? She would then change her role to the cash girl. She took this role very fucking seriously. She loved to take the money and separate the coins into the till. But she didn't like giving back any change. 'Amy, love. Give the kid his 65p change back.'

'Why, Dadth? It's ours now.' That's my girl. You fucking tell them.

The guy I was working for, Steve, not a bad guy but a bit of a prick. The kind of prick that, let's say you're having a pint in the pub, standing at the bar on your own, just relaxing in the convivial atmosphere. Then you see Steve enter the pub. You would pick up your phone and pretend you were on hold to the tax office. Sorry, Steve, hello and shit, mate, but I am just on a call. I may be some time. Please feel free to fuck off and sit on your own. Steve was a big hairy fucker too. Sort of gorilla-ish type hairy. His arms were out of control with hairs. Thick black fucking things.

He was training me up on the rounds, teaching me the route and showing me how to make an ice cream and shit. He tried to show me how to make an ice cream boat one day. Boy, did he get a nautical fucking nightmare from me. 'Paddy, chill the fuck out. It's not a real boat.'

'Yes, I fucking know that, Steve, but still. Even in the midget world, that thing is not seaworthy. Its centre of gravity is all to fuck. Overload that at sea and you would get a negative GM. The metacentric height would rise above the position of G and you would have negative stability. It would capsize, Steve. That's all I am saying.'

'Paddy, just fill it with fucking ice cream, mate, please.' Oh my days. What's wrong with these people?

'I just hope, Steve, that the customer isn't planning on eating this in the bath. If they expect this to remain upright, then they have it all wrong. An ice cream Mayday, Steve. An ice cream Mayday, mate. If it's a big, fat fucker that takes it into the bath, he will create a tidal surge similar to a tsunami. That boat won't stand a chance. Carnage, Steve. Utter carnage. There will be flakes floating about with hundreds and thousands clinging to them, trying to stay afloat and clinging on for dear life. Ice cream Mayday, Steve. Ice cream fucking Mayday. mate. I will say no more.'

I remember him on this particular day. He was making an ice

cream for a customer. I was watching him closely, as if I were some sort of ice cream pervert. Anyway, this fucking hair drops off his arms and onto the ice cream, you couldn't miss it. Big black hair on a white backdrop. So, I saw this and was expecting him to chuck it in the bin or at least flick the hair off. Nooo; what does the dirty bastard do? He covers the fucking thing in strawberry syrup and hands it to the customer.

'Steve,' I said. 'There was a dirty great big fucking hair on that ice cream that fell off your arm.'

'Yeah, I know, Paddy. Sometimes that happens. You can't start fumbling about and picking it off in front of the customer. Just smother it with syrup. The weight of the syrup sinks the hair into the ice cream.'

'Fuck, Steve. Why not just lob it into the bin and make another one? Or wear a fucking long-sleeved shirt or something?'

'Can't do that, Paddy. It's all about the profit and the image.' What a manky bastard. Maybe that's why ice cream is white, due to manky fucktards like him moulting all over it.

It was a cracking little job to be fair. It wasn't a deal breaker, that's for sure. I wasn't intent on making a career out of it. But it was pleasant enough. However, I still had this fucking thing of doing more in my head. Surely you can up your game a bit, Paddy? You are made out of strong stuff. You know you can. I was earning just marginally more than I was earning previously at the glasses factory. I could supplement this with something, couldn't I?

So, I got searching again and subsequently got an interview for a huge warehouse, B&Q, in Runcorn. Now this place is the hub, if you like, of B&Q's North West division. It supplies all the outlets in the North West with whatever that outlet has ordered to fill its shelves for customers. The job role was order picking, driving around this huge place on them pallet trucks. Not a fork lift truck. A pallet truck. You stand on the back of these things. They have two forks in front of you and you just basically drive this around with either a pallet or a couple of baskets, a bit like a shit sort of Segway with two battering rams on the front. My job was to drop off orders from my assigned picking sheets to the corresponding loading bays, where a lorry would then come in to load up and ship it to the designated stores. Fuck me, I should have worked in logistics. Am I fucking good or what?

The hours, if I remember correctly, were ten p.m. to six a.m. (Ten o'clock at dark time, kids, until a time you will never see until you grow up and get some fucking responsibilities in your life. Yes, you. You little prick. Put the book down and go and help your mum with the dishes, you lazy little shit.) It was five days a week with, I think, weekend optional overtime. So, Paddy lad. You can do your ice cream shit of a day and this of a night. Sort of double your money for the family. Two saber-toothed tigers for you and Amy to cook whilst Emma can just watch, looking all pretty and peeling her perfectly round spuds.

It still wasn't offshore money. But it was a step towards it at least. Now, I can't remember the exact conversation I had with Emma regarding this. I know that it went along the lines of her being concerned that I was taking on too much. I did listen and discuss this with her. I was sober. Her opinion matters. However, I somehow convinced her that I would be okay, and all would be fine. If it was too much, I would simply stop it.

So, I would start my day at around eleven a.m. (All timings are estimated by memory; they may be exact. I cannot confirm this but it's as near as makes no difference anyway.) I would drive to the depot to collect my van then head out and complete my day's ice cream sales. The round was back-to-back, staggered over the day. So, essentially, I was hitting thesame stops twice in the one shift, albeit at different times. That's pretty fucking obvious, Paddy; if it was the same time then that would require a time machine, and if I had one of them, I wouldn't be sitting on this ship now, typing up this book. I would be tucked up in bed with Emma on the lee side of Bum Island.

After my round was completed, I would return my van and head home. I would then maybe grab a quick burger or something similar from a drive-through. I would arrive home at around seven p.m. to my two lovely girls and a freshly cooked meal. I would then make up excuses such as, I am okay, you know, Emma, really, I am full, I've eaten too much ice cream today, or something along those lines. I tell you what though, love. If you put that in the microwave for me, I will really enjoy that once I have finished in the factory. Yum, yum.

The microwave and I didn't really see eye-to-eye. You are a selfish bastard, you, Paddy. She opens up my door and leaves them revolting fucking, oh Paddy, there's not even a word for them. She leaves them inside me all night. Then you come home from work. Have a bowl of cereal. Open me up like I am just a tin of spaghetti hoops, take out the awfulness and then just chuck it in the bin. Yes, the bin, Paddy. What's the point of that, I ask? I remember a time, Paddy, when we microwaves meant something. Nuclear power, Paddy. Yes. Not just storage. You have that big, useless bastard over there for that, the fridge. Just sitting there like Mr Cool, all smug. Shut up, microwave, or I will get my screwdriver set out and give you a fucking yearly service. We all know what happened to Humpty fucking Dumpty, don't we? ALL RIGHT.

After chilling out with my girls for a couple of hours, I would then head off to the warehouse for my night shift. Once completed, I would then be back home for around six thirty a.m., slide into bed with Emma, attempt the wandering hand on thigh trick. If no resistance, then happy fucking days. Game on. If hand was swiftly removed, then game off. Fair game, then straight to sleep. Up again at ten a.m. and repeat the process. I was getting weekends to catch up on rest, I do believe. But it was hard going. Motivating myself was the hardest.

This was all good at first. I was managing to keep it together. The first few days were really tough, and then my mind just kicked into it and my body just followed. Not that it had a choice in the matter. I sort of knew that this would be the drill anyway, after working crazy, sporadic shifts throughout my career. After a few weeks though, it was time for me to throw the towel in. My confidence in my ability to maintain the schedule was outweighing my body's ability to continue.

I did recognise this risk; however, I did not manage and process it accordingly. In my haze, and combined with my underdeveloped mind management strategies, it seemed rational for me to continue on the premise that throwing in the towel was a sign of weakness, failure. I was actually starting to fight back the army of non-believers and debtors. People who had very little faith in my ability to succeed, or more to the point, my visions back then of the people who didn't have faith in me succeeding. Although now, upon reflection, these people never really existed. It was my mind that built up this barrier. And it would have been so easy for me to allay these feelings and thoughts with Emma, who would have rubbed them out. However, back then I wanted to do this alone and I wouldn't give in. I would stand and fight this army alone if I had to. I needed to do this for my family.

I finished my shift on this particular morning. It was fucking dancing down with rain outside. I was exhausted. I climbed into the car. Mirror, signal, manoeuvre, checking my blind spots for cyclists, and off I went. I was joining a carriageway. The entrance to this carriageway, like many carriageways, was up a slip road. This slip road was in a horseshoe type of shape, or half-horseshoe rather would be more accurate, otherwise you would come off that slip road pretty much next to where you started. Anyway, me being a bit tired, I sort of overcooked the bend a bit at speed in those conditions, and the back of the car started to overtake the front, and I spun a full 180° and ended up facing the traffic coming up the slip road.

Fuck me. I regained composure pretty swiftly and then pointed the car in the right direction and carried on my journey home. I knew that this wasn't right. It's because you are fucking exhausted, this, Paddy. Something has got to give here. I can't just give up now though, can I? Disappoint my family. Have those army of doubters and non-supporters smirking at me.

This moment in my life was a major turning point for me. It ended my identity as a family man. But I often wonder. What was it that made me come to the following decision? Was it the fact I had been sacked from so many jobs in my youth and now, somehow, I saw quitting as failure? Was it because I felt I was letting my family down by quitting? Was it because I felt it was weak of me to quit so early? Was it because of my imaginative army of non-Paddy supporters? Or was it simply because I had an urge for drugs?

I can only answer this by quizzing my past. Opening up those files of days gone and cross-referencing them with decisions I made whilst sober back then. Not decisions made whilst on the moon, as they are irrelevant to this particular question. The conclusion I have drawn is that it was a combination of all of the above. All factors above carrying the same weight and decision input as each other. Why are you including the urge for drugs as a factor that you can identify, Paddy? Well, simply because the following and final decision was made, signed and sealed far too quickly.

By the time I had left that slip road and joined that carriageway, I knew that I was going to be visiting a drug dealer later that day. My risk management was fucking pathetic. I knew it was risky for me to do this. I did not, however, successfully manage that risk, which in turn did not apply the necessary severity to the consequence analysis algorithm in my decision factors. It's the brain, people. Brains are processing plants. Just like fucking computers. Mine was an old bastard Amstrad back then. Just my hardware. Operator error, if you like.

People talk about the subconscious. I prefer to view the subconscious as a bowl connected to an array of filters, interchangeable filters that you can alter and move around if you understand the system and you know how to operate it. These filters trap the bullshit and the illogical, or they can in many cases trap the sensibility and the logic. What then passes through the filters and into the bowl is the subconscious decision. I am not fucking stoned, by the way. Just coffee in my system at the minute. It's two thirty a.m. LMT just here now in Norway. I am typing this from my own mentality. My way that I deal with my life these days. How I have had to uniquely identify this process and tailor it to me. You can search forever and a day, but you will not find what I have just written in any textbooks. This is my thoughts. My brain. My way. The end. In laymen's terms.

I had said to myself, Paddy, you are fucked. So exhausted. That's why you have skidded off the road. But you are stronger now, so just a little bit of amphetamines will help to overcome the tiredness. Just keep it controlled, as you now have the ability to do this. Your family need this. All bullshit that my filters were letting just slip through and into that big bowl of shite. If it's ever down to just you, which in life it often is, and you, just you alone, have to work the problem, then please use every fucking recourse to hand to enhance the dangers surrounding that problem and work out how to effectively rub them the fuck out before continuing. If you can't, then you need to apply the brakes until you have a solution. Turn around and head the other fucking way if you must.

So that evening, I visited a dealer and scored myself some speed. Right, only take a little, Paddy. The feeling I had once this drug was in my hands was a feeling of excitement, which backs up what I have just written about the urge and the shit in my bowl. The motion had already been passed before it began. It was a landslide fucking victory for the drug. That big bowl of shite just spun around like a tombola, mixing with all the other shite inside and crushing the logic. Sum total equals a fucked up subconscious decision.

I had reached the peak of my family man legend at that point. Never to return. A regret that has fucking forced me to understand why the fuck I took that risk. I was about to lose Emma as my fiancé and have a negative impact on my little angel's life forever. This is when I travelled below rock bottom. I reached that level and then smashed my way right through it and continued on down.

Guess how this drug started to impact on me? Yep. Slowly. As all drugs do. Like an orchestral symphony, it builds up to the crescendo. If it didn't and it just started suddenly at the crescendo, you would wince, wouldn't you? Woah, fucking steady on with that trumpet, you daft bastard, you scared the fucking shite out of me then.

In no time at all, B&Q North West had the fastest order picker in the West. I would be overtaking every fucker on my shit Segway. I would pick an order, and instead of dropping it at the drop off point, whereby a forklift truck would then take it onto the waiting HGV lorry, I would just bypass this point and go straight to the lorry. Beep, Beep. 'Paddy the Picker coming through, P.T.P., out of the way.' Beep, Beep. The guys driving the forklifts would just look at me, thinking, where the fuck's this lunatic going now?

I would drop off my load next to a confused-looking lorry driver. 'There you go, mate. My name's Paddy the Picker, P.T.P. for short. Nice set of wheels, mate. Fuck me, there're a lot of them aren't there? Imagine pumping all them up in one go with a bike pump, hahaha. What's the zero to sixty on your truck anyway, mate? Doesn't matter. Look, listen. If you need anything, like fucking lawnmowers or paint or anything, then you just put a shout out for Paddy, all right?

'Paddy the Picker, and if you run out of room on your lorry, mate, for your load, you can just throw it in the back of my car and I will drop it to the store after my shift. My back seats fold down and everything. I've got one of those portable parcel shelves in the back. Eh, imagine if you had a parcel shelf in the back of this wagon, eh, fuck me, it would be huge. Right, got to go. Don't forget. Ask for Paddy the Picker.' Beep, beep.

Eyebrows were starting to become raised at B&Q's management division too. 'Who is that daft twat over there?'

'Who, Mr Supervisor?'

'That fucking loon with "TURBO" painted on the side of his shit Segway. The one wearing a plastic sheriff's badge and shooting at people with a cap gun.'

'Oh, yes, Mr Supervisor. That's our new picker, Paddy. Just

look at him go. Boy, would you look at him go. God speed, Paddy. God speed.'

I was back up to crazy shit again. Every fucker would be taking their lunch breaks and here was me on the shop floor, polishing up the forks on my pallet truck. Nice and shiny, Paddy, nice and shiny. The smoothness and the shine will not only make your shit Segway stand out in the crowd, but it will also aid in lubrication when sliding in to retrieve a pallet, thus improving efficiency whilst maintaining the uniform.

I was also getting noticed at home by Emma. She must have been distraught, looking back. I am so sorry, Emma. My usual timings when sober were, and are usually, very accurate. I don't like to be late for anything. Even now, when I come to the bridge to take command of the watch, I am always twenty minutes early, just so the officer handing the watch over to me can do it in my time and not his. I just think it's courteous and polite. And I expect it to be reciprocated. If not we will have words. After that, it's fucking warfare. And you will lose. In the words of Ivan Drago, I will break you.

Anyway. I would usually be home by six thirty a.m., feed the bin with Emma's dinner then have a bowl of cereal, leaving a little bit of milk in the bowl and putting it on the floor for the cat. Even though we never had a cat, it's the thought that counts, isn't it? I would then be straight up to the nice warmed-up bed. Turn on the taps and test the temperature with Emma. (Sorry, Amy.) And that was that.

Now however, I was home by six fifteen a.m., pulling onto my driveway with my exhaust and brakes in flames. Straight into the house, into the shed and grab my tool box. I would then hunt for an operation. Right. Let me fit an extension to that hoover lead. All of the other electrical appliances fucking crying their eyes out, sob, sob. I really thought it was going to be me, I really did. I had been spared. Right, Paddy lad. That's a good job. Seventy-five-metre cable on that hoover now. No more of that changing plugs and shit around the house now, eh. Emma will be thrilled. Eh, Paddy. You could even start up a little business. Plug in the hoover and just stand at the end of your street by the main road and make a hoover stop for buses.

It was during one of these silly mornings that I was doing some essential kitchen maintenance, like steam cleaning the cupboards with an iron and a toothbrush or something daft, when I heard a noise upstairs. Shit, Paddy. Emma's getting out of bed. I had to change character, fucking like now. So I ran and jumped on the couch, bounced out of the open window and barrel-rolled under the car for cover, burning my arse on the exhaust. I jumped on the couch and pretended to be asleep.

Anyway, she came flying down the stairs. She wasn't a fan of walking, Emma. And then into the living room, where I was pretending to be asleep on the couch. 'Paddy, Paddy, Paddy,' she echoed.

'Ahhh, yawn. Morning, love. Ohhh, I was flat out then,' I said as I was rubbing my eyes as if just woken up. 'Are you okay, Emma? You look shocked.'

'Paddy, I had a dream that you were dead. It was so vivid in my head that I actually thought you were dead on the couch.' Now, can you imagine what I must have been putting her through? Her head was playing fucking tricks with her because she was up the fucking wall with worry. I remember that moment like it was yesterday. Her just standing there, looking all confused and hurt. She was wearing light blue pyjamas, short-sleeved with matching shorts. Little white dots on them. I felt so guilty.

'No, I am not dead, Emma. Just dead tired.'

138

'Oh, my fucking days, Paddy. The dream was amazing. We had a massive party for your funeral. There was jelly, cakes. Hot dogs with pineapple chunks on cocktail sticks. Sort of council estate kebabs. Champagne and everything.'

So, evidently now things were going the shape of the pear. The cunt within was awakening from the depths of my mind. Becoming stronger. Full of energy after its long sleep, but equally hungry for rot and terror. Crawling its way through the labyrinth of tunnels and defences that I had created over time to try and trap the demon. Its slimy webbed hands folding around the entrances of openings. It's huge cock dragging behind it on the gravel cave floors (well, we are related). Rays of light emitting through the cracks in the cave walls, exposing their weak points. The points to target. I could hear faint sounds as it drew closer. 'Paddeyyyyyyyyyyyyyyyy. Soon we will unite once again, my old friend.'

I can't really recall what happened with regard to B&Q. I think I just never turned in for my shift ever again. I imagine to this day that they have my shit Segway on a plinth, displayed in the main entrance of the warehouse, a gold badge with the words "P.T.P. The man. The Legend" on full display. Also, the same written in fucking Polish and Russian and Bulgarian and Romanian for the UK's general workforce of today.

That cockiness was well and truly back. 'Fuck this, I am not going back to that place, Emma. It's a fucking joke. I am going to concentrate on laying some turf down in the spare bedroom and making a miniature crazy golf course. Amy will love it. You have no say in any matters any more. So, go and boil a fucking lettuce or whatever the fuck you throw on the plate and call food.' So with that, I took the easiest route. I stayed on the ice cream van. There was no boss there except me, right? I even stopped

Amy coming with me. Why? Because now, Paddy, it's all about you. AGAIN.

Now. Let me enlighten you on how an ice cream van operates. You have the van. Inside of that van is the ice cream maker. I don't mean me, I mean the machine that makes the ice cream. Now, without that machine, you are just basically a man in a van. And if you stop to speak to little kids in such a fashion, you will swiftly get your fucking head kicked in by an eagle-eyed, suspicious group of parents. Quite rightly too. Or you could phone the police and they will ascertain shit for you, which they are quite good at doing.

So, this ice cream-making machine that I am referring to basically turns the vanilla liquid that you pour into the top into the ice cream that comes out of the bottom via the process of freezing and churning. The freezing is basically just the same simplistic design as your home domestic freezer: evaporator, condenser, etcetera. The difference on an ice cream van is that although the principle of the freezing is the same, it is supercharged, if you will, by the belt that is driven from the van's engine. So, it therefore freezes dense liquids, such as vanilla and full fat milk, in no time at all. It then churns it, and the product from the pump is whipped white stuff.

Now, the amount of cash/earnings estimated per day of an ice cream van's rounds is determined by the amount of vanilla liquid left over upon completion. Basically, the vanilla mix is supplied in five-litre drums. Each of these drums, on average, equates to fifty pounds' worth of ice cream sales. I would take three of these five-litre drums out per day, or more accurately, Steve would supply me with three per day.

Therefore, for example, if I were to return after my day with 2.5 litres of vanilla mix, the owner, Steve in this case, would estimate that I had made roughly one hundred and twenty-five pounds on ice cream sales alone. The ice lollies, confectionary, tinned drinks, etcetera, were stock counted. The ice cream is estimated. The cone wafer count is irrelevant because they are so brittle and break all the time; they jump out of the boxes when you hit a speedbump. They are just sacrificial elements in this equation. So that's how they operate.

When I first started on the ice cream van, I got chatting to a lad called Dave. A nice lad to be fair. He had been doing the ice cream vans for twenty years or so. A real career-minded type of bloke. He used to work for Steve and like me was of the same opinion, which was, the man was a prick. Now, Dave passed onto me the secret of the ice cream man's con. The ice cream man's guarded secret. The magic circle of the flake pushers, if you like. Now I am going to reveal that secret. Paddy the Whistle Blower. Every time an ice cream van passes me from now, I will just hear 'You fucking grass'. Fuck you anyway, you pricks, you rip off kids and you load boats up all wrong.

Here is that secret. Milk. Fucking milk, Paddy? Are you taking the fucking piss? I pulled this fucking book closer to my face to keep this secret to myself and all you say is fuckin milk? No. I just said, milk. I didn't use foul language. That's the secret, honestly. Full fat milk will freeze the same as vanilla in the machine and will come out whipped, just like vanilla, out of the pump, albeit without the taste and a lot whiter.

So, by mixing milk with the vanilla, the owner cannot argue that takings of the ice cream sales are low, not when you are bringing back the vanilla. You just had to ensure that all the milk was flushed through the system when you returned the van after the shift, because sometimes Steve would beat me to work. He owned two vans, one that he drove and one that I drove.

However, occasionally he would clean out my machine if he made it into work before me. I know a lot of people will be shocked. Paddy, you robbed the poor kids. Nooo, I never. Calcium, people. Milk is full of it. Healthy bones and shit. I was doing it for the kids. Honestly.

So, I would stop at a petrol station at the start of my rounds. Ten pounds of diesel and a four-pinter of full fat milk. On two separate receipts, of course. I was coining a nice few quid extra threw this scam, which was assisting towards the purchase of class A drugs. This however, in no time at all, also started to get out of hand. I was arriving late for my rounds. Missing out stops. Fiddling with stuff in the van I shouldn't have been fiddling with, for example, the box that played the Popeye tune. I took it apart to investigate its inners, maybe jazz up the sound a bit. I subsequently killed Popeye. So, I spent that day creeping up and down the street, leaning on my horn to signal my presence. That last sentence sounds a tad weird, but it is fact.

Let's fast forward a few weeks. I was now at that manic stage. Crazy fucking bastard once more. I would disregard everything and anything poor Emma tried to do or asked of me. Speaking down to her and everybody else. I remember her asking me simply, once, 'What time are you due back tonight, Paddy?' A perfectly reasonable question, eh? Nooo. Why the fuck is she asking me this? What gives her the right to keep tabs on me? Why won't she just leave me the fuck alone? She is constantly on my fucking case.

'Emma. I will be back when I am back, for fuck's sake. I will bring you a fucking Curly Wurly back with me. Fuck's sake.' Nag, nag, fucking nag. She never fucking stopped, fucking GBH on my ears. Paddy, when are you back? What do you want for your tea? Paddy, are you okay? Paddy, do you want to talk?

What's with all the fucking irrational bullshit speak? What's your point, caller? Just leave me be.

I was getting really angry with the public on my rounds too. I pulled into this small cul-de-sac one day. I parked the van up outside somebody's front drive. I stood up and began to prepare my cornets and shit, switching on the ice cream machine. Now, this machine was pretty loud inside the van, and it was difficult to hear much above that noise. Next thing, fucking bang, bang, bang on the driver's window. For fuck's sake, who is that? I opened the window, and it was a lady, looking all pissed off and annoyed.

'What's up, love?' I said. She pointed, sort of behind her. I couldn't see what she was pointing at, but she then just started shouting at me. 'My husband and I have been beeping our horn at you for the last couple of minutes to move this fucking van out of our way so we can get to our driveway.' Now firstly, she has ruined my first impression of her. Lady. Ladies don't speak like that. I just looked at her and told her to piss off. I then carried on arranging my cones and shit. Next thing, like the fucking exorcist, she is at the serving window.

'I have just told my husband what you have just said to me and here he comes now.' I flew out of the window like a mad man, nearly knocking her over. Then straight over to her husband, who was walking towards me from his car.

'You fucking cunt, come here you twat.' The poor guy just dropped his arse where he stood and ran back to his car. 'Stay in that fucking car, you horrible cunt, and you, fucking blonde-haired foul-mouthed bastard. You get in the fucking car with him. I will move when I am ready to move. You pair of cunts.' I don't think they expected psychopathic ice cream seller. I don't feel bad about that moment at all if I am honest. I would have called him a cunt sober if he was so impolite. I probably wouldn't have bailed out the van, dribbling from the mouth like a fucking bull terrier though.

Another occasion shortly afterwards, it may have even been the same day, I can't really remember, I turned a corner and hit that Popeye tune. I passed a lad pushing a pram and then parked up. Machine on and arranging my cones again. Next thing, 'Oi, you.' Now, I fucking hate that word; it makes the hairs stand up on the back of my neck when somebody addresses me this way. 'Your fucking bell has just woken up my baby in the pram.' What do you want, dickhead? A free ice cream?

'Fuck off, you stupid cunt.' Next thing, this guy, trying to appear hard, sort of jumps up and puts his face right into the van from the serving window. I was going to bite this fucking cunt's nose off pretty sharpish. I put my hand on his face and launched him out of the van, arse over tit over the pram and onto the floor. 'You cheeky fucking cunt. Try that again.' My point I am making here is that my aggression was attracting aggressors, like a set of cunt magnets, if you like. Pulling each other towards each other.

The milk-to-vanilla ratio got out of control. The poor kids in the end were just licking blue top milk. 'Eh, mate. Your ice cream doesn't taste of anything.' Fuck's sake.

'Give me it.' I would just smother it in strawberry sauce and sherbet powder. 'There you go. Now piss off.' I was returning the van in the evenings with hardly any wafer cones and a load of vanilla. 'Sales were shit today, Steve.'

'Where're all the cones, Paddy?'

'Fuck's sake, Steve. I fed the fucking birds, all right?' I knew he was going to get rid of me any day. So, one day shortly after this, I took the van back, emptied the takings into my pocket, helped myself to half of his stock and just left him a note calling him a cunt and telling him he would get both barrels if he turned up at my door. Sorry, Steve. You feed people hair ice creams. You rob the kids and give it to yourself. You are no Robin Hood. You are a cunt in my eyes.

CHAPTER 18
Armed and ready to rob

Now, before I continue with this, I would just like to add, if there are any police officers reading this, and you are trying to ascertain if there is a charge involved, by process of ascertaining, just read the title, dickhead. Confession. You haven't got me, and ascertaining is not necessary. It's not about me or you. It's about my loved ones and the truth. So do your worst if you want to go down that route. Stick me in jail again. I could do with a break and a catch-up with my mates anyway. Life will go on, and I will continue writing. My highly paid job will still be there for me upon my release. And you, my little Porky Pie, will continue apprehending and ascertaining all day long.

I had lost any credibility that I had clawed back. I had once again become an absolute fucking mess and a joke. I was a total disgrace of a man. I had sunk my family once again into further debt. But did I care? Yes. Of course. Could I work out where that care should slot into this fucking torrent? This tempest of a fucking storm engulfing my mind and churning my emotions? Nope. Not one bit.

Where I come from. Where I live and hale from. Liverpool. I fucking love the city and the people (to a degree). The term in Liverpool for somebody who is addicted to amphetamines is whiz head. That's what I was. A whiz head. Now, whiz heads come in many shapes and forms, ages and classes. But all whiz heads will affect the same sort of mannerisms. In any major city's outskirts, districts, if you like, if you were to drive up or down a

146

residential street at three a.m. in the mornings, and if on that drive you observed a downstairs light of a house on fully (not lamp lit, I mean full-ceiling fucking one thousand lumens light bulb fucking Pink Floyd concert lighting rig lit up), and if you continued this drive for a week down this road at the same time, and on six of those days, that very house is lit up, that's probably a whiz head's house.

If it's an upstairs light in a bedroom, then it's just probably a fucking flake who likes to sleep with the lights on, or is too scared to turn the lights off, would be more of an accurate statement. But I fucking guarantee, if you could see inside of that house, you would probably observe a man or a woman, or both, trying to invent the new jet engine using thirty second-hand hair dryers tied together with cable ties. The latter doesn't even work to be honest, it's too noisy and the fuse will keep blowing.

Honestly. I can spot them from a mile off. Always a bit paranoid, bizarre sense of humour. Sitting on a train doing a crossword, breathing heavily as if they have the Readers' wives page open in the *Razzle* wank mag. Ooooo, Betty, forty-seven, from Bristol. Fine set of top bollocks, Betty, I must say. Loose the nipple ring though, love. I would do fucking crazy mad shit myself. Fucking ceramic wall tiles on the ceiling. Fuck me, Paddy, the ceiling looks like the floor, and the floor looks like the ceiling. Now when you lie on the couch between projects you will feel as if you are floating upside down. Send a picture to NASA, Paddy. They might adopt the idea for their mission training. You might even get a go of a space shuttle. No need for a sat nav, my fellow astronauts. I have been up here many a time, I know the route.

This is right across the board with whiz heads. See a girl pushing a three-wheeler pram with stabilisers retro-fitted. That's a whiz head. See a guy on a pushbike with a car's alternator taped to his handlebars and a wire running into a dynamo. That's a whiz head. See a rather dashing, well-dressed, sexy-looking bastard of a man in front of you. That's just me. A whiz head will always be carrying a Swiss Army knife. In my case, as I was an upper class whiz head, I carried a Leatherman. Just in case you need to alter the time on your wristwatch. Nope, fuck that little winder thing on the side of the watch, Paddy. That's for amateurs. A spot of horology is required here. Take the back of the watch and reverse the gearing. Always the hard way.

One of my mantras, if you like, in my life, when approaching any sort of operation in my profession is **keep it simple**. What do I mean? I simplify the task at hand, eliminating all the bullshit. I get the views and suggestions from everybody directly involved and the views of the people who are not involved. Why does an outsider's opinion matter, Paddy? It's simple. Their train of thought is not with their own individual role in the operation, simply because it doesn't exist. They will see the whole picture. Remember I said earlier, an observer will always see more of the game? Well, that's the logic. Keep it simple, using all available inputs. Filter out the bullshit and I guarantee you success. That is my way.

Again, it's my way of successful leadership through common grounded respect, knowledge and experience. The frame of mind I am in just now is fucking awesome. I love it. I am just on absolutely fucking everything. Ahead of my game, calm and settled. We are departing Bergen, here in Norway, in the morning. Nine a.m. LMT. Out to a survey site in the North Sea to begin sub-sea surveying for the oil and gas sectors. I am all over this. The crew is briefed, up to speed, everybody is happy and sober. Positivity fucking rains down own my crew. They love to be here. We are a big family.

The heads at the top of this tree know what we are doing, we are on top of our game, and we understand that it's the crew that run the ship, not just one jumped up little underqualified fat fuck. Clueless little bastards on ego trips. Yeah, you know who you are. Cunts. If I were to take speed again and become that whiz head, things wouldn't be like that here. It would be a circus show. 'Paddy. Why are all those massive telegraph poles lying on the deck?'

'Well, my mate. I am going to drill a shit load of holes on both sides of this boat. We will use those poles as oars and fucking row our way across the North Sea. Just like the Vikings. Paddy Bennett. Mr Energy Efficiency 2021. The world will love me.' Especially those eco fucking vegan annoying twats. Like that girl, Greta, I think her name is. Crying her eyes out over emissions and the ice caps and shit. It's a product of the age we are living in, you silly bitch. Why don't you just piss off and go and cuddle a fucking penguin? Move in with them. Or better still, Greta, go and hug a fucking polar bear and then see if you're still concerned about them being wiped out after that.

To be fair, you would probably just fucking bore it to death anyway, with your blinkered views, dwelling in the realms of your own fantasises. I should take her on a trip out here and let her see how much emissions these oil and gas platforms churn out of their flare booms every hour. Get a fucking job, girl, and give your head a wobble. Maybe get your hair done and get a facial. You are only playing to a limited audience anyway. The only ones that listen are the fucking fantasists like yourself. Rant over. Truth be told I couldn't lead a swarm of flies to a pile of shite on that gear. But I would believe I could. Now that's fucking powerful stuff, people.

Poor Emma and my baby girl were beside themselves. I was now out of control. My family were trying to step in and help but it was useless. It was falling on deaf ears. I sold our family car at the auctions just to get money for more drugs.

'Paddy, where's the car?'

'I sold it, Emma.'

'What do you mean, you sold it, Paddy? How am I supposed to get to work and back?'

'Fuck off, Emma. Leave me alone. I will buy you a fucking Space Hopper and you can bounce your way to work.' I know, people. What a horrible cunt, eh? Speaking of cunts…

'Padddyyyyyyyyyyyy,' sniff, sniff. 'I am free from the caves. I am yours once again. Your oldest friend has returned. I have gravel and stones in my bell end, Paddyyyyyyyyyyyyyy. Dragging this huge cock for many leagues. I did this for you and me.' Fuck off, cunt, you scumbag. Leave me alone. 'Paddeeyyyyyyyyyyyyyyyyyyy. I see that you are down. But we are not out.' Sniff, sniff. 'Trifle for a tan, Paddy. Trifle for a tan. Now I must rest. Sleep, sleep, sleep, sleep, sleep.' Oi, you fucking cunt. Don't you fucking dare, you lazy bastard. Gone. What does it mean? Trifle for a tan? Trifle rhymes with what? Hmmm. Rifle. Yep, I have an air rifle. Tan? Rhymes with, oh hang on. Van. Rifle and van? Rob the fucking ice cream van. Oh, cunt. You are sooo naughty, you really are.

The assault weapon in question. A .177-calibre single shot split barrel spring-powered rifle. The type that you get in the fairgrounds to shoot a tin duck and win a goldfish. Makes a noise similar to a forced fart. Sort of, phhhfffttt. It's not going to scare away the Taliban, but it could crack the shell on a snail's back from two metres. Speaking of snails, or the snail-related family, I once owned a taser. Yes, a real one, Mr Officer. You cannot ascertain anything about this, Officer, because like everything else electrical, I took it apart and fucked it.

Anyway. I was curious. I wanted to taser something. Pets were out of the question because I am an animal lover. So I tasered a fucking slug, didn't I. Yep, unfortunately for me though, due to the slug being slimy and wet, a return voltage travelled back through the stun torch and into me. Yes, I fucking tasered myself. It didn't half hurt too. Anyway, my rifle, after hours of trying to adapt it into a machine gun, was fucked. You basically had to load the pellet into the barrel end, a bit like a musket gun. You then had to maintain the angle just above the horizontal at all times, otherwise the pellet would simply just fall out again. A real combat weapon, it was.

So, Paddy. Weapons check? Roger. Ten-four, rubber ducky, confirmed and checked. Disguise? Right, Emma's knicker drawer, pair of tights, confirmed, checked. Attack and escape vehicle? Shit, I've sold my car. I will borrow one from my mate, confirmed and checked. Attention all call signs. THE QUAILS ARE IN THE NEST. I say again. THE QUAILS ARE IN THE NEST. OUT.

Now, it's always 'OUT', people, or 'OVER'. It's never fucking 'OVER AND OUT' like you hear in the movies, or the fucking security guard in Pound Land. In correct radio telephony terminology, OVER equals the invitation to reply or please come back to me. OUT equals end of transmission. I have finished speaking with you. So, by saying the words 'OVER AND OUT' during communications through R.T. (Radio Telephony), what you are essentially saying is, please come back to me, I have finished speaking to you. In the same fucking sentence. You have contradicted yourself. Although I don't blame the Pound Land security guard in any way. If you pay peanuts, you get monkeys.

The end. It was more just a bit of trivia for you keen paintballers. Or the Territorial Army. The S.A.S. as are they are known. Saturdays and Sundays.

I borrowed my mate Kevin's car. Obviously, he didn't know why I had borrowed it. A bit shitty of me when I think back. But hey, me and risk. I wasn't going to borrow Emma's Space Hopper, now was I? She loved that thing.

So, the tactical plan. I was armed. I was off my fucking rocket and I was good for a go. I knew the route of the ice cream van in question. His last stop on his way back to the depot was on the grounds of a particular mental hospital. He would drive in, play his tune then do a three-point turn at the end of the road and then park up, facing the entrance that he had come in. A one-way street, you see. One way in and one way out. I would park up in my attack-and-escape vehicle near to the entrance/exit.

I had a spotter, that was myself, keeping eyeballs out for him. Once he came around the corner, I would duck down out of sight, assault weapon laid across my legs. It was fucking huge, this rifle, too. It went right across the width of the car. Not ideal for close quarters combat. Anyway, he would play that tune, turn around and park up. I would then roll the tights down, covering my face, reverse back then jump out with my assault weapon. I would run up to the serving window looking all aggressive. 'Give me a fucking ninety-niner now, loads of sherbet and strawberry sauce on it. With two flakes.'

I was going to run up to the serving window. 'Hands up and give me all of your fucking money.' No, hang on, Paddy. He can't do both, can he? He can't put his hands up and give you money at the same time. You are asking him to do the impossible there, Paddy. Not unless you are expecting him to frisbee you twenty-pound notes out of the till with his cock. No. Just run up to the window, Paddy. 'Give me all your fucking money. And a can of Fanta. Sugar free.' Yeah, that's better, Paddy.

I got myself into position. Comms check. Paddy. This is you. How are you reading me? Over. Loud and clear, Paddy. 5/5. Over. Roger that, Paddy, we are standing by. Keep comms light. Out. Right, Paddy, weapons check. Rifle in position, safety on, locked and loaded, full metal jacket. Operational camouflage, Paddy? Confirmed, tight on head, ready for the roll. Attack-and-escape vehicle, Paddy? Roger, keys in ignition, handbrake off, gearbox in neutral, petrol in the red. Shit. Petrol in the red. ALL CALL SIGNS, this is Paddy. Petrol is in the red. I say again. Petrol is in the red. Over. Roger that, Paddy. Standby for confirmation to abort. Over. Roger, copied that, standing by. Out. All call signs, it's a negative on the abort, I say again, negative on the abort. Over. Yeah, Paddy the baddy copied that. Out.

So, I am now all pumped up, flowing with adrenalin. Just waiting on the package to arrive now, Paddy. Let's hope it's a go. Any minute now. All call signs. Target vehicle is in range. It's a go. Out. He then came into sight, Bugs Bunny and Elma Fudd clearly visible on his bonnet, identifying him as the target. All call signs. I can confirm. I have eyes on the package, eyes on the package. It's a go. Out. So I ducked down. I let the van pass me as planned. I got up again. Shit. There was a woman and a kid just turned the fucking corner. Shit. All call signs. We have friendlies in the vicinity of the package. I say again. Friendlies present. Stand down. Please acknowledge. Over. Yes. Copied that. Rifle One standing down. Shit. I ducked down again. I was not about to traumatise a poor woman and her kid. Not at any cost.

By the time this dozy woman has passed me so had the ice cream van. Shit, Paddy. You will have to hit him near to the depot.

So I followed him. We stopped at a set of traffic lights. I was immediately behind the van. A car stopped next to me. I was looking straight ahead at Daffy Duck's beak on the van's rear. But you know when you can feel somebody staring at you? I looked across at the car next to me. The guy behind the wheel just turned away quickly. That's odd, I thought. I looked at Daffy again. Then I could feel it again. So, I looked across at this guy again, and he was just staring at me, with a sort of astonished, dozy, gormless bastard look on his face. I will never forget that look he gave me.

Anyway, I shouted across, 'Who the fuck are you staring at, dickhead?' The guy just shat himself and then attempted to merge his car with the one in front of him. The lights changed and we pulled away. Checking my blind spots for cyclists, I then thought, hang on, Paddy. When you just shouted at that bloke, you sounded a bit odd. Sort of nasal. Almost as if you have a cold. Oh shit, you fucking daft twat. You have the tights pulled down over your face, the other leg just dangling from the side of your head like a fucking satin earring.

That's how hyped up I was. It just didn't register. My nose was spanning the fucking width of my face. Fuck it. I was not backing out now. I kept on Daffy's arse all the way to a particularly long and deserted road near to the industrial estate where the van's depot was. Now or never, Paddy. He who dares, lad. I pulled out and overtook this van, got in front of him and slammed my brakes on. The cunt just indicated and went around me. What a cunt.

Take two. I overtook this prick again and threw a belter of a handbrake turn. Spanning my way across the road, I then jumped out of the car together with the rifle. The fucking pellet fell out of the end, right in front of me. Shit. He hadn't seen that. So I started running towards him, shouting, 'Give me your fucking money.' What did he do? He started fucking reversing. For fuck's sake. I didn't have a contingency plan for this. I continued chasing him up this road for fifty metres or so. He was just getting smaller and smaller by the second. Fuck. Abort, Paddy lad. Back into the car. Shit. There were quite a few flaws in your plan there, Paddy lad. Not exactly watertight now, was it? Ronnie Biggs would not have approved it anyway. I was looking forward to that can of Fanta too.

I was trying to make light of the above, people. It was of course an awful thing to have done, and I am deeply ashamed of myself for doing it. I probably traumatised the poor guy involved, and for that I am deeply sorry, although I like to think that he probably laughed about it, told his mates in the pub, 'Eh, listen to this. This fucking dickhead...' It was nothing related to the hairy prick Steve either.

Not long after this and after causing a whole load more trouble, all authorised by the cunt itself, Emma finally had enough. 'Paddy. You have to go. It's finished this time, for good.' So, what does Paddy do? I took an overdose. Now, the pills I overdosed on were dihydrocodeine, a very strong painkiller derived from opium. Proper strong, they are. They were in a drawer upstairs. They belonged to Emma's late grandmother, Pat. A lovely lady, she was. R.I.P. Pat.

I knew that these tablets wouldn't kill me. Of course, I did. I am the encyclopaedia of drugs. Fucking walking Wikipedia on such topics. I know them all. However, Emma didn't know that I knew this. I wanted her to feel sorry for me, take pity on me and let me stay. So, I took a shit load of these things and dropped on the couch in my best acting fall. 'I just don't want to be here any more.' Fuck, Paddy, get your lines right, for fuck's sake. We rehearsed this. You do want to be here. That's why you took the tablets. Get it right, dickhead.

Take two. 'I want to be here. Sob, sob. But I don't want to live any more. Sob, sob.' Silence. Is anybody even behind me? If she has fucked off and walked away, then that's just bang out of order.

'Paddy. I am phoning an ambulance.' Oh, good, she's there. Eh, Paddy, I wonder if they will put the blue lights on for you? They might even send the rescue helicopter. Yeah. How fucking dramatic would I look? By the time the medics arrived, I was off my fucking trolley. Off my bastard tits. I remember thinking, oh, I like these. I hope she doesn't throw them away.

The medics tried their best to revive me on the settee but I just played dead. They placed me in a wheelchair with a nice tartan blanket across my legs. I threw my head onto my shoulders and hung my tongue out of my mouth as if to signify the final moments. I remember having an itchy arse too. I couldn't just get out of the wheelchair, scratch my arse and get back in, could I? CUT. The medics wheeled me into the back of the ambulance. There was no room in the front. I remember the medic, once the doors were closed, saying to me, 'You can wake up now, mate, we are away from the house.' Cheeky bastard, I thought. I am nearly dead here.

We arrived at the hospital. My cock started itching, and then it shouted up to me, 'Hey, Paddy mate. Where are we, mate? This place smells familiar. Oh no. Oh no, no, no fucking no. Not again Paddy, please no. Don't you fucking dare let those three psychopathic bitches near me again, Paddy. I will throw your fucking balls at them, Paddy. I swear I will.' Calm down, cock, for fuck's sake. It's nothing to do with you. 'Hahaha, fucking hell, Paddy. You made my eye wince. Eh, Paddy. Whilst you're on. Where is Emma? I haven't played in the lady garden for a few weeks now. You just have me doing squat thrusts these days.' I am working on it, cock. Shhh, leave me to chill and enjoy the drugs now. Speak later. Love you.

I vaguely remember my mum and my sister visiting my death bed that night. They were of the same opinion as the doctors: he is wasting our time, the fucking idiot. I had a load of discs attached to my torso. They were just stuck on with sticky-type adhesive. Around three inches in diameter or there-abouts. They were hooked up to a machine that monitored vital signs. I looked the part anyway.

However, when I awoke the next morning, fresh as a daisy, these things had disappeared. Shit. Where had my props gone? I had a quick mooch in the bin and recovered them. I fucking needed those for later. I was discharged, and then I went straight home. The house was empty, apart from the kitchen appliances letting out a quick scream. Fuck, he is back. I knew it wouldn't last. Farewell, Ninja Juicer. It was nice knowing you, said the Breville.

Right, Emma will be home soon. I must get back into character. A few rehearsals and shit. So, I stripped off and jumped into bed, leaving the cock on the floor. 'Give us a bunk up, please, Paddy.' Fuck's sake, stop pissing about, cock, and get in the bed. Emma will be back soon. 'Whayfuckinghey, I knew you weren't lying, you old dog you, Paddy. I am going foraging.' Calm down, cock, and shut up. I am trying to concentrate here. So, I am lying in the bed, pads back on my torso, albeit not connected to any machine. Well, they don't use real bullets in the movies, right?

In came Emma. 'Emily. Cough, cough. You came. Come closer, my love. Let me see your face.'

'Paddy. Get dressed. And get the fuck out of the house now.'

'But Emily, I can barely walk. I am weak.'

'Well, how the fuck did you get back from the hospital then, dickhead?'

'Erm. I was teleported.'

'Paddy. Just go, please.'

'Okay. I will leave. Farewell. I love you. I don't suppose you have got any of those tablets left, have you?'

'FUCK OFF.'

So off I went, back to the parents, blaming everyone and everything around me.

CHAPTER 19
The first sentence

The phrase 'know yourself' is not to be taken lightly. My dad would often say this to me. Know yourself, son. You've got to know yourself. I would often sit in my bedroom, staring at my passport. It is me; what the fuck's he talking about? It's a rule, a standard that you need to understand to run and manage your life successfully. Some people can, along with a lot of other key life elements, develop this early. In my case, like everything else, it came late in life. That is my belief anyway. Why are you telling us this, Paddy? Simply because it's my fucking book. So, I can.

I do however know myself now. I understand why I did what I did, did what I done, whatever. Writing this book, for me, has been a balance of controlled emotions. There is a shit load more in my head, but I can't get access to that because my switchboard is protecting me, I believe. It is only allowing me to have what it thinks I can take and manage. I need special Paddy-type approved software installed to access such memories that my switchboard is protecting me from. I know I sound a bit like one of those I.T. fucking techno knobs here, but like I said it's my fucking book.

So, I am now back in with the parents. This time however, I had no intention of giving up the drugs. Deep down, I knew it was the end with me and Emma. You cannot put someone through the levels of emotional heartache that I put Emma through and expect them to remain at your side. Again, I understand this now. I blamed her at the time, as if it was her that was broken because she couldn't help and repair me. Like I mentioned earlier, it's your job to fix yourself, with the exception of the poor percentage of us that do suffer naturally with mental health and depression. Those people really need the care. The rest of us are born with sound functionality and hardware. It's our own doings that lead us down that slippery road, and through our own doings we must recover from this.

It's too easy to blame somebody else for your mistakes. That's why we do it. It's the easy way out. Just a little tip here. Think a bit more about the other person in the equation, how they are feeling and what they need. It will help you to know yourself.

With this, I went in the opposite direction. Me and cunt united as one to cause as much fucking destruction as we possibly could. I was making phone calls to Emma with threats, leaving her horrid messages, driving up and down my former road at all hours, making her feel scared and threatened by me basically. This was all with my baby girl inside of the house too. Allowing my daughter to see her mother scared of her father. I know. What a fucking man, eh? Time machine, people. I tell myself often enough, one day, Paddy, I am going to come back and batter the fucking shite out of you. Although I also believe that if time travel were something of the future, then surely someone would have been back by now to tell us about it, wouldn't they? This is that level that I mentioned earlier. Miles below rock bottom I had travelled, and I continued, down and down.

Emma finally called the Ascertainers, who then came out with their notebooks and ascertained stuff. Actually, I shouldn't say that. I will give the police the level of respect they deserve for dealing with such fucking scumbags as myself back then. If it weren't for them intervening, then God only knows what may have happened. So, thanks to the police for protecting Emma and

Amy in this case, boys. That is without sarcasm. Thank you. I was initially given a police caution and informed that the next step was court. So, shortly afterwards, I appeared at court and was warned by a judge to stay away and to do the right thing. Fuck him. Fuck the police and fuck everybody. I just wouldn't listen.

It happened once more. I was taken to court again. I was arrested on the Friday afternoon. I was a bit abusive and erratic whilst in police custody, so they wouldn't interview me or whatever. So, the following morning, I was taken to court. It was Saturday morning at Liverpool Magistrates' Court. Unusual for a court to operate on a Saturday, but anyway, it did. I remember being held in the cells underneath the court, coming down off the moon and surrounded by a load of fellow scumbags. Dirty junkie fucking house-robbing fucking scumbags. I remember looking down upon them. Stay over there, you horrible cunts, or your jaw is going to be snapped in half. Looking back though, was I in a position to judge? No, was I fuck. I deserved to be in amongst them, let's have it right.

I was remanded into custody to await a further court date. HMP Armley in Leeds. All the fucking way to Leeds in a sweat box. A prisoner transporter van, the white fucking horse box-type vans. These things are not designed to transport the clients contained within in any sort of luxury. Horrible fucking things, they are. There are individual little cells inside, with a plastic seat and a small window, just so that you can observe your liberty disappearing from you on route to prison. I have been in quite a few of them over the years.

However, for some reason, the one that I was transported from West to East in had a horrible fucking mesh design on the plastic seat. My poor arse was getting pounded. That's the only pounding that this here fine arse is going to be getting too, Paddy, whilst incarcerated. I will go out in a blaze of blood if any fucker tries to make me play mummies and daddies in here.

We arrived at the prison. I had just turned thirty years of age. A bit too old to be experiencing your first prison sentence. I started to feel quite emotional as we were ordered from the wagon and into the reception to be processed. 'Off the wagon, you lot, and into reception to be processed.' That's how it went down. No fucking way was I showing any fucking emotions in this place though. Show a little and it gets exploited fucking rapidly. Anyway. I had the Q&A session. Then I was taken away for searching, etcetera. They gave me this fucking awful deep purple tracksuit with white flakes all over it. Really not my colour.

I was ordered by a screw (prison staff, cunt) to undress and squat. The squatting is to see if a parcel of drugs or a phone will drop out of your shitter. I was then then ordered to get a shower. He was fucking worse than Emma, this cunt, with his do this and do that. I bet you he gives me a hoover in a minute. So, I got into the shower.

'Eh, mate. Officer. Is there any chance you can do my back for me? Maybe give my neck a little rub? No, seriously though, Officer, does my arse look like a waffle? If there're any pimples on it, we can have a game of *Connect 4* whilst you're waiting.'

'Just hurry up, you cheeky cunt.' I finished my shower and got dressed. He could fuck off if he thought I was putting on somebody else's underpants. I got dressed in this deep purple with white-speckled design tracksuit and looked in the mirror. Fuck me. I looked like a tin of corned beef.

I was then allocated a cell, together with a cellmate. My cellmate was some old guy. I haven't a clue what he was inside for. I wasn't really interested to be honest. There was fighting over the top bunk, put it that way. The fucker wouldn't have made it up there without busting his hip. I remember just lying there for a few minutes. The comedown. Emotions. A plane flying overhead. Back to that bedroom as a child. A happy place. My holiday to Spain. Janet's tits. I fell into a deep sleep, deep enough to sleep the clock around for over forty-eight hours.

I woke up feeling fucking awful, the realisation of where I was hitting me instantly. Plus, my fucking arsehole was stinging like mad. I looked down the bed and my corned beef tracksuit bottoms were just hanging of one ankle. Ouch, you bastard. I must have slept funny. I pulled up my trousers and turned around. The old guy was just sitting on a chair with his feet on the bed. He was smoking a cigar and blowing smoke rings up towards my face, just smirking.

'Fucking pack that in, you creepy old bastard. What time is it?'

'I am sorry, son. What was your name again? I didn't quite catch it the other day.'

'It's Paddy. Paddy the Baddy.'

'NO, IT'S NOT, IT'S BITCH. NOW GET THOSE FUCKING TROUSERS BACK DOWN AGAIN AND BACK ON YOUR FRONT, YOU MAN SLAG.'

He told me I had slept solidly for a couple of days, scaring the shite out him with my shouting random shit in my dreams. Fuck. I was on a major fucking comedown now. I felt a bit hungry. 'Eh. Creepy old bastard. Where's the phone? I need to call reception and order a continental breakfast. Do you know if the sausages here are locally sourced? Or are they shop bought? I wonder if they have a vegan option?'

I was full of all kinds of emotions at that stage. Those bastard clouds were doing their shit, bouncing all over my head. A day or so later, I was taken back to Liverpool to be put in front of another judge. This judge bailed me from court under strict conditions regarding contacting Emma in person, by telephone or via a third party. Ah, what about a pigeon, I thought. The Romans used them for carrying messages. Pigeons were the first texting service. My parents had also had enough of my antics. My mum threatened to ground me for a whole month if I didn't stop being naughty. Fuck that.

The drugs started again immediately. I hadn't really detoxed enough in the short few days of involuntary withdrawal. It had, to be fair though, been a welcome rest. A much-needed rest. Now my reign of cuntness could continue.

Emma's poor dad, Rob, had taken ill again. He was back in the hospital. I did care. Of course, I did. I was very fond of Rob; he was a fucking great bloke. However, in my head, this was not about Rob. Or Emma and Amy. Or fucking family. This was about me and getting what I wanted. Now, you know I mentioned earlier that the environment of being at sea on a ship doesn't lend itself to drugs in my case? Well, neither does living with parents. Don't get me wrong, my parents are cool enough and good company. But with drugs, noo. My mother is the anti-Christ and my dad's a moaning prick. I needed to get away from them. I felt trapped.

All I had to do was drop the drugs, but I wasn't ready or willing to do this. I didn't have a car. My mum wouldn't lend me hers, because she was protecting me. She knew at that time that the first stop in that car would have been at Emma's. I saw this as my mum just being an awkward bitch. Also, Emma wouldn't let me see Amy. Why? She was protecting her. I would never harm my daughter, although I felt like booting her up the arse the other week when she said, 'Bye, Dad. Love you,' then jumped in her car and fucked off, leaving me all those dishes. Emma knows this. But that's not what she was protecting her from. It was her seeing her dad in such a state.

Things were just getting on top of poor little Paddy now. Everyone was just so against him. The poor, wounded lad. I needed freedom. I needed to flee from there and get myself and the cunt mobile again. But I didn't have a car. And no fucking money. I know, I will just borrow some. So, with that thought process locked and loaded, I stole my mother's credit card and went to the car auctions.

He was back with a vengeance. Paddy the cunt rides again. Re-born and ready to rule once more. Jack of all trades and master of none. A legend in his own lunchtime. All the gear and no idea. Get your filthy paws off my silky drawers. Just ignore that last one. My wings had been unclipped and I was as free as a motherfucking bird again. I was cutting about the streets and up to no good in this car, thanks to my mum's credit card. Two thousand five hundred pounds, tasty little Audi A4 2.5 litre V6. A little rocket ship for the rocket man. Well, I did deserve this, didn't I? I mean, if people would just wake the fuck up and see that this was all about me, then maybe we would get somewhere. Until then, until they came to their senses, I would just continue. Obviously, I was not going back to my parents' house. My mum would surely ground me after this. Fuck that.

I knocked at Peter the oddball's house one evening for a catch up. His dad answered, holding his daughter's hand in one hand and a banjo in the other. Then Peter appeared. 'Yo, Peter. Woah, you are still a bit of a whiffy bastard, aren't you? How's life? Have you finally got yourself a woman? Doesn't matter. Look, lay down banjo, take that harmonica out of your mouth.

Lose the dungarees and the lumberjack shirt and come for a drive with your old mate, Paddy.'

'Oh. It's a bit awkward just now, Paddy. It's family orgy night. My brother is just oiling up my grandmahhh as we speak. Unless, Paddy. Would you like to get involved?' Suddenly, all the banjos stopped playing and all the family inside of his house just turned around to face me, smiling, teeth missing. The ones that weren't missing looked like they were covered in a yellowish, greeny-black coating. His dad spat into a steel bucket, making a sort of 'spidingeee' noise.

'Erm, thanks for the offer, guys, but I am more of a flute and fairy-tale man myself. C'mon, Peter, let's go.'

So, we got in the car. 'Nice car, Paddy. How do I close my window, mate?'

'Erm, that's broken, Peter. You have to keep it open, let the air in type of thing.' His mate was in the back of the car too. This twat was the most annoying fucktard that I have ever met in my life. He just wouldn't stop laughing, at nothing. He was like one those Furby fucking fluffy toys the kids used to have. Just giggling all the time. Sorry, that's going in the fucking bin, I remember thinking, this cunt's is not right in the fucking head. I was sure he was on some sort of drug. I was going to pull over in a minute, drag him out and punch fuck out of him then check his pockets, because I want some of this action.

Anyway, roughly about thirty minutes later, after the pleasantries, I dropped him and the Furby back off at his. 'Right, there you go, give my love to your mum, Peter, not literally, I mean verbally, and put a fucking muzzle on that prick next to you before he loses the function of his jaw. Tatty bye now.' I pulled away and closed all the windows. Oh, I thought, it's fucking nippy in here. Within those thirty minutes or so of driving around

166

with Peter and the other daft twat, he had told me about how well he was doing, all of the savings he had accumulated of the years. Tens of thousands of pounds. **Cue the cunt.**

'HHmmmmmmmmmm, Paddeeyyyyyyyyyyyyyyyyy.' Sniff, sniff. An interesting wealthy little fucker of a friend you have presented to me there. HHmmmmmmmmmmmmmmmm.' Fuck off, cunt. I didn't present nobody to you. Anyway, cunt, why do you always fucking appear whilst I am having a piss? You're a fucking gay pervert, you are. 'Paddeeyyyyyyyyyyyyyyyyy. We have an opportunity to attack. The mere mortals are at the castle walls. They are threatening to overthrow your reign. We must act now, Padeeeyyyyyyyyyy.' I will tell you what, you scumbag. Why don't you just whip out that massive cock of yours, charge at them and fucking windmill the fucking lot of them?

A few days later, I was still out and about. I was sleeping in the car sometimes, or resting, rather, as I only needed three-second yawn every three days to keep going. This car had electric folding seats. How nice. Maybe I could steal the electrical motors from the seats and fit them to the engine somehow to make a hybrid? I would have to look into that. Then some nights I would stay at a mate's, although when he went to bed, I would stay up and jet wash his electric cooker.

'Paddy, what the fuck have you done to my fucking cooker?'

'I know, mate. I knew you would be happy. It's spotless, isn't it?'

'It doesn't fucking work, Paddy.'

'Ah, yes. Well. Your microwave fits in the oven, I have already checked. So, if you put your microwave in the oven and close the door, then that's sort of roasting shit, isn't it?'

I was running out of what little cash I had scammed fairly rapidly. I would have to sell the car. The world's first Audi A4

2.5 litre V6 Hybrid would just have to wait. Shame. I knew that was going to be a winner too. I sold it to a guy for one thousand pounds and an old Mondeo, same colour and model as my old one to be fair. This cash only lasted a couple of days though. I was snorting vit C like a mad man. I did invest a small sum though. I am not stupid. I bought an air pistol.

Now. Back to Peter. As a kid, I remember him being tighter than Scrooge himself. He would not part with one penny. He actually used to keep his money in his underpants or his mum's knickers or whatever the fuck he was wearing, because he knew that only the boldest of knights, Sir Lancelot himself, would only be brave enough take on such a noble quest as to rummage around Peter's plum sack looking for the prize. So he wasn't going to just lend me money. I had to use force to take it.

He had told me where he was working whilst on our drive. The cunt already had the GPS co-ordinates mapped out for me. So, I went to do a bit of reconnaissance, a recce. I parked up at his factory, in the car park, right next to the main entrance, a slightly unorthodox approach to surveillance, I must admit. I had been parked up for some time, observing by means of just looking, the people nipping out from a side door for a cheeky smoke. He must be out soon. Come on Peter. Fag Break.

Next thing, I got this awful waft. I knew that smell. There he was. He was standing right on the corner. Game on, Paddy lad. I climbed out of the car and rammed the pistol down the front of my trousers, the cock reacting immediately to the threat. 'Paddy, Paddy, oh my fucking days. Help me quick. Some fucker's pointing a shooter at me.' Calm down, cock, it's me. 'But why, Paddy? I haven't done anything wrong.' No, I don't mean it's for you, daft fuck, it's for someone else. 'Phew, oh dearie me. Paddy, hahahaha, you give me a fucking fright then. Make sure that safety's on mate, please, or I will lose my one and only eye. Phew, I need to lay down after that. Hahaha, you're a crazy bastard you are, Paddy. Pheww, hahahaha, you fucking nut job.'

I approached quietly, on all fours, like a tiger stalking its prey, my shoulder blades moving up and down methodically like a pair of slow pistons. Then he saw me. 'Hello, Paddy mate. What are you doi…' He caught the evilness in my eyes and just fucking bolted. I bolted after him.

'Come here, you little cunt.' Through the door and into the factory I was chasing him, pistol in hand, around pallets stacked with boxes. It was like a scene from Benny Hill. I was getting dizzy. Fuck's sake, that lad could corner like a fucking housefly. Then he just disappeared. Gone.

Where the fuck had he gone? Honestly. It was like he just pulled his lip over his head and swallowed. Just vanished. That was the second time this twat had done this to me. I stopped and checked my surroundings. Where the fuck was he? He was not on my back, was he? The fucking workforce were just at a standstill. Mouths open wide in amazement.

'He has got my fucking fishing rod and he won't give me it back, all right? Fucking cunt.' I walked out of the factory and back into the car. Where the fuck did he just go? Well, that was another armed robbery fucked. I did apologise to Peter a couple of years ago for this on a particular media site. He replied with, 'Don't ever contact me again' and then blocked me. I think he is still bitter. I am really truly sorry though, Peter. You are a legend for not grassing me up. Although it doesn't really matter now, as I have just confessed.

I was getting fucking desperate now. I needed cash. And I needed it now. Not just twenty or fifty quid. I had notes rolled up all over the car. I needed the product, not the paraphernalia.

There is a grocery shop I used to occasionally go to, for groceries, funnily enough. That's just how I roll, people. The dimensions/layout of this place are around ten by five metres, with a shelf-isle type of thing down the middle. It stocks a wide range of gentleman's reading material too. I only like them for the art. Honest. Now, I have visited this shop a fucking lot. And there is only ever one guy working behind the counter at any time of the day or night.

The night Paddy burst through the door with a set of tights on his face and a pistol in hand, there were fucking three men working there. Shit. I only had one pellet. The rest were in the car. There were two guys behind the counter and one was stacking the fridges. Fuck it, I'm here now. 'Give me all of your fucking money. Now.' My brain was digesting my odds, fuck me, Paddy. You've got to think out of the box here, mate, think unconventionally and do it fucking fast.

Next thing, whooshhhh. A fucking tin of a certain zesty drink went flying past my head. Fuck me. He's was using his stock as missiles and his arm as a sling. What sort of warfare was this? This wasn't fair. I'd heard of food fights before but this was fucking dangerous. Did he realise I was not wearing a helmet? Whooshhhh, another one. Fuck me, Paddy. Bail now. Save yourself. If he upgrades his rounds to a tin of fucking Whiskers and that bounces off your head, then it's good-night Vienna, my mate. So I bolted out of the door and back into the car and off I went. You have a lot to fucking learn about this armed robbery shit, Paddy lad.

Right. T.O.F.T. (time out from thieving). I fucking hate that, you know. Another thing that annoys the shit out of me. Names given acronyms. What's wrong with just using the words themselves, you lazy bastard? W.C. (water closet). R.I.P. (Rest in

Peace). (R.S.V.P.) Reply and a bit of French. N.O.R.W.I.C.H. (Nickers off ready when I come home). That's all you ever needed. Nowadays, every fucking industry is using them. I worked with a guy recently. He would annoy the fucking shite out of me with this.

'Right, Paddy. I have completed the T.B.T. and P.T.W. for the operation ahead. I have explained to the guys that this is a C.P.T. operation. Now, the R.O.V. will be L.A.S.P. at around 09:00 U.T.C. According to the I.M.D.G. code and M.A.R.P.O.L. regs, combined with S.O.L.A.S. and C.O.S.W.P., it should be smooth sailing. I have added the old, be the tool in the box and not the fool in the box to the guys involved for the kick off. Is that okay, Paddy? Any questions?'

'Erm, no, mate. I understood every fucking word of that. You crack on.'

'Okeydokey then. Thanks, Pat.'

'I've told you, don't fucking call me Pat. It makes me sound like a girl.'

'Oh, I do apologise, Paddy. Right, see you shortly. T.T.F.N.'

'Yep. F.U.C.K.U.' Fucking gobshite.

I don't really get annoyed at trivial shit any more. I just sort of chuck it in the irrelevant filter and let it fade out. There's no point being a whinging bastard. Life's for living and enjoying. Give those miserable bastards a wide berth; they will pull you into a world of gloom. Negative twats.

However, I do get a bit annoyed with little things such as technology. Now, I wasn't a child of the technological age. I wasn't born into it. It's something that I have had to learn and adapt to over time. Computers for example. I have no problem operating them. The bridge I am on now is like something from *Star Trek*. It's full of systems, and I can operate and understand them all. What annoys me is when they try to effect the mannerisms of a human. Take my laptop. I switch it on. The buffering circle appears with the words 'Please wait' underneath it. Fair enough. I will let you have that one.

Now, if I hit a key on that laptop, another message appears. 'Just one moment please'. Grrrr. I fucking hate that. Who the fuck are you talking to, you ignorant bastard? If a barman spoke to you like that in a pub, you would drag the cunt over the counter, wouldn't you? The two sentences mean the same fucking thing. Please wait, and just one moment please. I will open you up and piss all over your circuit board in a minute, you horrible bastard.

Then there's the HDMI lead. Try plugging one of those bastards into the back of a TV that's hanging from a wall. Oh my fucking word, it makes you feel like you are stupid, like it's laughing at you. The prick who invented that is just a cunt in my eyes. There must have been much better designs than that. But they chose his. Why? I will fucking tell you why. He has something on the guy who approves the design. A bit of blackmail. He has a picture of him fingering a chicken or something. 'If you do not approve my design I will put this photo of you abusing poultry all over social media.' Grrrrrr.

I have wound myself up now. If such people fucking knew how shit I was at repairing electrical appliances, like a sort of, crossed-eyed surgeon giving you a heart bypass, then they wouldn't be such utter cunts. ALEXA. Fuck off. I hope your tits fall off.

Let's get back on track, people. Concentrate, Paddy lad. So I then decided to stash the weapon. Give the Ascertainers something to do if they caught me. I then cranked up the inner cunt. I would just drive up my road. See if there was a queue of burglars waiting to break into my house. Yep, right. You just keep telling yourself that Paddy, you scumbag.

I pulled into my road and saw immediately that my house, together with Emma's sister's house over the road, was just crowded with her family. I drove through them slowly, the protectors making a dive for my car. Fuck this. I was in no condition to be slugging it out with anyone just now. I needed my weapon. With that, Emma was straight back onto police HQ.

She now had police distress priority for all available Charlie call signs to assist. (Fair play to the police once again for this.) So, by the time I retrieved my pistol and found a lump of timber, the area was swarmed with police. They were searching for a pair of eyeballs driving a green Ford Mondeo.

I was just around the corner from my home, in attack mode, when I was T.P.A.C. (tactical pursuit and containment) by the police. Although the pursuit bit wasn't actually in it, as I was stopped at traffic lights. They didn't even give me a headstart. How unfair.

I was subsequently slammed into bracelets and taken to a lovely little quaint B&B, where I was charged with possession of a loaded firearm, breach of bail conditions and harassment and threats to kill, although the latter charge was later dropped through lack of evidence. But as this is fessing up time, yes, I did threaten to kill. So, it was back to jail again. This time, Paddy my boy, it was for a real sentence. I was still at that time convinced though that it was me who was the victim in all of this.

A short time after this, Emma's father, Robert, sadly passed. Gone but never forgotten, Rob. You were a true gent and a legend, mate, and will always continue to be. Y.N.W.A. I am so, so sorry to all the family. The wife, Anita, a lovely lady, the kids and grandkids. I didn't mean to steal these final moments with your husband, dad and granddad from you with my own being. I can only hang my head in shame for this.

To the shopkeepers. I am also truly ashamed and regretful of my actions on that night. I hope I didn't cause you all too much trauma. Maybe the three of you should however consider chipping in to buy a dart board. Hone in on that throwing technique a bit. Just a thought.

CHAPTER 20
Does prison work?

Does prison work? The word work is lacking clarity here. Does it work towards rehabilitation? For the majority of inmates, no. For the minority, yes. Does it work to maintain and install the correct tools required towards drug abuse? For the majority of users, no. For the minority, maybe. Does it work towards, as it proclaims to, providing a structure and a degree of balance in your life? Educate you? Furnish you with practical and academic skills? Unless you went into jail as a proper fucking fucktard? Then no. Not at all. It's a fucking circus, run by fucking clowns. I have respect for the judges who commit the inmates, I really do. But the prisons themselves are just like holiday camps. Better than holiday camps if I am honest. There are drugs on fuckin tap. Everywhere. And I have been in five of them.

I have worked on both the academic and the practical courses offered by Her Majesty's prisons. Both on this sentence in fact. During my next long sentence after this, the prison themselves supplied me with the drugs which very, and I mean very, fucking nearly cost me my life. Scumbags. But that's coming up later.

So, here is me. Opted in for some education in prison. Maths was the subject. I like maths, because I understand it. Maybe I could bring something to the table. Then again, no, Paddy. Just keep your fucking mouth shut and act dumb. You may as well paint an arrow on your arse cheek showing the direction to the starfish if you are going to act as if you are educated. John has five cocks and Bill has two. Nope. That's not a game I will be playing. Anyway, they start everybody off at the same level. There is no such thing as a personal induction to determine if you have any knowledge. They just assume that as you are a prisoner, then you must be as thick as pig shit.

The first lesson was addition (adding up, kids). Now, if you were to give a prisoner a piece of paper and a pencil, with the idea being that he is to write down the answers to an equation, just like school, then you could be faced with a bit of a dilemma. Firstly, the prisoner could be dyslexic and/or just dumb as fuck and doesn't have the ability to read and/or write. Secondly, you have effectively just supplied that prisoner with a weapon when you handed him a sharp pencil. Third is a combination of both the above, with an increasing danger that now the prisoner will become frustrated or paranoid with his lack of brain matter and then decide to help himself to a bit of yours, through your ear canal.

With that being said, some fucking idiot in the prison service (ninety-nine percent of the cunts) decided that learning mathematics through a computer game would be the best option. Each prisoner had their own computer in the classroom. The said computer was already switched on, and the game was loaded ready to go. The game in question was tailored to what most men like. Cars. If you like prams, then you should be on a different wing, you sick fuck.

Anyway, you drive one of these cars on the game using the directional arrows on the computer keyboard. Up, down, left and right. Don't patronise me, Paddy, I fucking know what a directional arrow is. Shhh. Don't interrupt me. This car you are driving is in the countryside somewhere. I sort of guessed that with the amount of fields and trees and shit.

176

Now, on this drive, a big fucking circle appears on the road ahead. Your job is to drive this car through that circle. Above this circle is the sum '3+5=?' Once past the sum, you continue your drive for another couple of miles, giving you a good five minutes or so to work out that sum. Reminders flash on the screen every few seconds, '3+5=?' Then, two circles appear on the road ahead. One has '8' above it and the other '92' above it. Your job is to drive that car skilfully through the answer you think is correct for that sum.

I got three correct on the bounce. I was just all over it, people. Anyway, this fucking idiot of a teacher just comes right behind me and pats me on the back. 'Well done, you. You really know how to add, don't you?' Patronising fucking prick. Where's that pencil whilst I stab this cunt up? All the other prisoners were looking at me suspiciously. Is this lad a grass? How can he know so much? Is he an undercover screw? On second thoughts, rule that out. There is no way one of those thick fucking cunts could have got three right on the bounce. Maybe undercover police. If he says the word 'ascertaining' fucking once, I swear he will be yomping on the bobby tonight.

The practical side was even worse. I first wanted to work in the woodwork shop. I had the skills, people, and with my abilities to fashion a shiv from a mere ice lolly stick, I was bound to become a huge hit. The master shiv dealer. However, I couldn't get security clearance to work with nails and hammers and shit at first, due to my status. So, they decided I could work in the denim factory, making jeans for prisoners all over the country's prisons, working with the Stanley knives and the razor-sharp scissors.

Are you now starting to get my point about the prisons being run by fucking halfwits? I am surprised they can even make it into work, the braindead bastards. That's why they have that massive one key fits all. Give these dumb fucks two keys and their heads would implode. When I was finally cleared for the woodwork shop, it wasn't what I was expecting. You just spent the whole day dodging nails and wood that were being thrown about like fucking missiles all over the place whilst the supervisors stayed behind toughened glass windows in a locked room, looking on with a cup of tea in their hands. Anyone observing this class from the outside would think it was a fucking dance class with the moves you had to bust out just to dodge shit.

The drugs in jail. Well it's pretty fucking obvious, isn't it, eh? You bang lads up for drug dealing on the outside. What are they going to do on the inside? Again, not thought out. I have seen first-hand. Lads coming into to jail fucking clean as a preacher's sheets and then leaving prison as a raging fucking junkie. Is that monitored or controlled? No, is it fuck. How do you control this, Paddy? Fucked if I know. I drive boats for a living. I can tell you one thing though. The whole system needs knocking down and re-building again, adding a bit of sense and sensibility.

My jail however was different. I did my own jail. I made it work for me because I wanted it to. I didn't want or need any help from these fucking morons running it. Just feed me and fuck off. Go back to your staff room and you can all continue trying to get that triangle shape through the square hole. To be fair though, the cooking was a vast improvement on Emma's cuisine.

I was in HMP Liverpool. STLP16 was my prison number. It was just one big fucking social club run by the prisoners. The screws don't run it. They couldn't run for the bus, those cunts, with the exception of one officer. (Yes. You know who you are, D.S.) The rest just operate the key. Lefty loosey, righty tighty. Or is it the other way around? Oh, I can't remember. We have just done a six-week intensive course on this too. Lefty, erm, lefty. Ohhh… Half of my mates from school were in the jail too. I've never hugged (man-hugged) so many men in my life. Yes, your freedom and liberty are taken away to a degree. But for me, I enjoyed it. It was a good laugh with a good ambience. (That's ambience, kids. Look it up. It's not something you go to fucking hospital in.)

In short, it was just what I needed at that time. I was again drug free. Strong and ready to be released back into society.

CHAPTER 21
My first command

So, for the fact that I had been a good prisoner. Ate all my dinners and got my sums right, ignoring the cockroaches. I fucking hate them things. When the screws turn the lights off on the wing, they are just absolutely fucking everywhere. Crawling all over the tables in your cell, up the fucking walls. Just everywhere. Insects in general don't really bother me, such as spiders and shit. I will often pick up a spider and sit it in my palm, just chat away to it. They eventually get bored and just trundle off. I don't understand why people are so scared of them, I think they are lovely creatures.

Speaking of insects, and in true Paddy style, slightly off topic, I have to share this. My mate Keith and I were just chilling on the couch one day in his house (a couch each, by the way). It was a Sunday and we were both just fucked from partying. Anyway, I was watching this ant running in sniper's nightmare formation on the laminate floor. So, I picked it up and had a little chat to it.

'Look, mate. Years ago, mine and your people didn't really see eye-to-eye. I may have hurt your race a little bit. Some may say I was a mass murderer. I don't agree with that. I warned you all at a very early age that robbing my jam wouldn't go without payback. Water under the bridge now as far I am concerned, Andy. That's your name now. Andy the ant. I am truly sorry, my friend. As a sign of peace and to further celebrate your christening, and additionally the ceasefire between our kinds, I would like to have a drink. Toast to the future, Andy.'

Keith just looked at me with one eyebrow raised like, fuck's sake, Paddy, you fucking loon. I took the top off a vodka bottle, poured a tiny bit of vodka in, just sort of wading, up to the bollocks height for Andy, and then dropped him in. I then took a pull of Keith's joint and blew that in too. I kept my hand on the top for a few seconds to keep the smoke plus Andy contained. And then I emptied it onto the table. It was fucking epic. Andy just walked in a perfectly straight line and then just fell into a groove and fell asleep. About an hour or so later, I just caught glimpse of him climbing out of the groove and staggering off. Job done. A big shout out to Andy the ant. Quits now, eh?

Anyway. So, I was released from jail with bail conditions. No more freaking people out, no more firearms. 'That includes fireworks,' said the P.O. (Principal Officer. The biggest of the pricks).

'Does that include safety matches?'

'Don't take the piss, Patrick.'

'Yes, boss. Whatever you say, boss.' The fucking leach. I was released into a bail hostel in Aigburth, Liverpool. These things are sort of a step below an open prison. It was full of alcoholics and drug users, all nice enough lads to be fair, as I remember. I however had my strong head on. All I wanted to do was spend a bit of time with my baby girl. Emma, bless her, would drop Amy off with my parents, and I would then go to play with her there for a few hours. Just playing games and having a giggle. Slowly though, so as to not overwhelm.

I had no fucking intention of going back to the drugs at that stage. Fuck that, Paddy lad. Never again. This hostel in question ran a curfew. If I remember correctly, it was around eight a.m. to ten p.m., and you had to attend the weekly day's activities planned, rock climbing, go-karting and shit. All good fun. It was certainly a step in the right direction anyway.

I wanted to get earning again though. Proper money. I was still unsure about going back to sea, but I was going to stick my toe in the water. Pardon the pun. Anyway, a good mate of mine, Captain James Kavanagh master with Irish Sea Ferries just now, another legend of a bloke, he was at this time working as captain on fuel tankers. These vessels operated out of Liverpool. Their primary role was providing fuel for other vessels, such as ferries, cargo vessels, you name it. No, not submarines, you dickhead. I was speaking with him, and he told me that the company he was working for were searching for a new master for their fleet. I had never been captain before. I have never wanted to be if I am honest. But I can lead a crew. I know my trade and I am a very confident and competent ship handler. Fuck it, let's give it a go.

I attended an interview. I flew through said interview, obviously leaving my criminal past and current address out of the Q&A session. That's the thing about my rank when starting a new job with a new company. My level of rank never goes through the criminal background checking system. They just assume that somebody in my position isn't, or has never been, involved in a crime. Until now. Oh my days. 'Okay, congratulations, Captain. Welcome aboard.' Happy fucking days. I could still do what I was good at and what I loved doing but stay at home. Best of both worlds.

I worked as a shadow master for a couple of weeks, just to get a feel for how these vessels moved. The vessels I had predominantly operated on prior to this, in rank, like the one I am sitting on now whilst typing this, they have multiple propulsion systems. Bow thrusters, stern thrusters, azimuth thrusters, CPP controllable pitch propellers. Huge twin Becca rudders with 70°

limits on them. Basically, once you understand the principles of propulsion and you know how to apply it, you can basically make your ship dance the dance of a ballerina. The difference with these tankers I was starting on was that they are what's known as single screw, or one x fixed, either left- or right-handed propellers with limited rudder, with no forward thrusters. It makes them very difficult to manoeuvre, especially in ballast, or lightship (without cargo). It's all about the transverse thrust, people. You know what I am talking about?

It was a great job. The problem I had was the curfew in the bail hostel. It was impacting on the job and the hostel's terms. The thing about these bail hostels is that they have the power to send you back into prison in a heartbeat, should your breach your conditions in any way. Basically, you cannot take the piss. In the few weeks that I had been a resident in this hostel, prior to getting this gig on the tankers, a few of the supervisors had asked me the same question. Why are you here, Paddy? Not that they knew anything about my profession. It was because I wasn't the average sort of resident to pass through. I am not singing my own praises here. I am not like that, and furthermore, I detest people that are like that. We are all equal as people in my eyes. It's the same with my crew. The steward here is just as important to the vessel as me. We are a team here. We all have our role that defines the word 'crew'.

I spoke with the hostel's manager, Mike. He agreed to release me from the hostel and let me move on with life. I moved back in with the parents for the time being. It was good for me to be there, sober. It worked. My mum doesn't drink; she eats like a horse though. But if you even try and give her a glass of water, she will just rear up on those back legs and bolt over the fence. My dad doesn't drink now either. The parties they have these days are fucking awesome.

I was working staggered days on the tanker. The crew were all local lads, so nobody sort of lived aboard the vessels. There was adequate accommodation aboard, but no one wants to stay on a ship when they are only twenty minutes away from home.

There were three types of fuel that we were suppling, three fuels commonly used in ships. They were IFO360, IFO240 and straight diesel. IFO360 is very dense. When heated, it is a dense liquid, but when cooled, it is almost like tar. Therefore, it needs to be at a constant, or above a constant, temperature for it to remain pumpable, or transferable, to the receiving ship. Basically, we cannot pump tar from our ship to another ship. It must be liquid. The latter fuel is used by very large vessels such as super tankers, which will use the heavy fuel for ocean passages and then switch to a lighter fuel when land falling, or hitting the coast, mainly for emission regulations but also because the engines are more responsive to the lighter fuel. IFO240 is the same as 360 but lighter. And diesel, well, it's just diesel. Now, bear with me here. There is a point to all of this.

So, my vessels operated on many various factors, the two mean factors being, A: none of the vessels had heated tanks. Therefore, for example, if I was supplying a ferry with IFO240, I would need to load my vessel from the heated storage silos on the quayside, straight into my vessel's tanks, by means of various large fuel hoses connected to various manifolds and large pumps. This took generally around two hours to load, let's say, one thousand metric tons of fuel onto my ship. Once this fuel had been loaded, it would then effectively start to cool instantly due to me having no way of heating it up. Therefore, the longer the fuel remained in my cold tanks, the thicker it became. Then it would reach a stage whereby it was too thick for my pumps to be

184

able to effectively transfer it to the customer.

Now, that's where factor B comes into play. The tide. It comes in and out twice a day. That's all thanks to the moon and gravity. Now, you are sitting all cosy in your garden after a barbeque, everyone has fucked off home and you are sitting, relaxed, with your partner. You look up at that beautiful backdrop of stars and the moon, trying your best to be romantic and sincere. Now, the stars and the moon are not put there for this moment, for you to have your wicked way with the Mrs. They serve a purpose.

The stars are where all the spacemen live and the moon is where you get your cheese from. When you look at the moon, and if that moon is round shaped (like a football, kids), then that means it's either a full, or a new, moon, which in turn means that the sun is in line with the earth. Hence no shadowing. Now, when you have a half moon, or a quarter moon (half of half a football), this means that the earth is at a right angle to the sun, or an angle of thereabouts. The moon is effectively being shadowed by the earth and sun's rotation combined.

Are you back on the fucking weed, Paddy? No, I am not. It's relative to this story. To conclude. When you see that full, or new, moon (twice a month), there is more gravitational pull exerted on the earth. And that gives you what's known as spring tides. The word 'spring' in this case has nothing to do with the season spring. It means spring as in trampoline spring, boyyunngggg. The gravity is at its most at this time, having a springing effect on the oceans, compressing them more and pushing and pulling just like a spring. Therefore, the tides are fucking rapid and powerful. When the moon is half or quarter shaped, then that's what's known as a neap tide. The spring effect through gravity is a lot less, therefore the tides are a lot weaker and for shipping, a lot more manageable. Thank fuck I got that out of the way. Planets tomorrow. Ten thirty sharp.

Where's this fucking relevance to the above, Paddy? You nearly killed me off then, you boring bastard. Well, here it is. I had to take these two main factors into consideration and try to make them work for me whilst operating my vessel. I was operating on the River Mersey. If the tides are too low, 9Spring or neap dependent), I would simply have to wait. If the tide was high enough in places, I could depart. The strength of the tide, i.e., the current, is down to my professional discretion and judgement. The captain's call, if you like.

Now, believe me, the River Mersey has one fast-flowing fucking ruthless current on high water springs. Always take great care with any river with your children and pets. If they happen to fall in on the wrong time, at the wrong tide, then it's sad to say that you alone will not have the ability to recover them. It's the same with these daft twats on yachts. We mariners call them WAFIs, or wind-assisted fucking idiots. They leave the harbour in their yachts, wearing their red Regatta jackets, khaki shorts, sandals and aviator sunglasses, looking all smug and overloaded with pomposity. Next thing, Mayday. They do not fully understand that you are floating on a constantly moving surface. Just because the water looks still, it doesn't mean that is the case underneath the surface.

So, that's what the job entailed. No nine to five. All factor based. And all depending upon commercial requirements and additionally environmental conditions and restrictions. The usual and practised drill was that two crewmembers would arrive at the vessel a couple of hours prior to the planned departure. One would work from the silos on the quayside, pumping the fuel from the various storage tanks. The other would stay aboard the ship, opening and closing various valves and manifolds on the deck to load the ship's tanks. It was a standard two-man operation. Then I and the remaining crew would arrive approximately thirty minutes before departure. I would complete the necessaries, and off we would pop. We would complete the operation and then return the vessel back to port, shut down and then go home until the next scheduled departure.

We would all take the loading of the vessel in turns, including me, so that it was fair to all crew across the board. So, just to summarise, if we were departing at five a.m. for example, I and another crew member would arrive at the vessel at three a.m. if it was our turn. We would then load the vessel together, and vice versa, yin fucking yang.

On a particular morning though, it was my turn to load. So I arrived at the docks. I then boarded my vessel and began firing up all systems and shit. Still no sign of the second man though. Where the fuck was he? So, I phoned him. No answer. Fuck's sake. So, I waited and waited. Still a no show. I was in a bit of a pickle here now. I needed to get clear of this dock and into the locks that I had pre-booked so that I could get onto the River Mersey on the flooding tide (tide coming in). If I missed the flooding tide, it would then go slack (tide on the turn) and then it would start ebbing (tide going out).

Now again, on this particular morning, the moon was the shape of a full football. What did that tell me, people? The tide heights/ranges and current/speed was going to be at its most. It would impact my vessel's ability to get up to the required speed on the river heading into an ebbing tide, which meant I would be late for the ferry I was due to supply the fuel to, which would then put the ferry and its passengers behind schedule. Knock-on effects, that's the commercial pressures that a captain is constantly under. It's not just looking out of the windows, eating fish fingers and smoking a pipe. So, I was now under pressure. I had to make a decision as the captain. The book essentially starts and stops with you. I had to make that call.

My call was to load the vessel myself, which didn't exactly go as I planned. With my rushing back and forth to the silos and then back to the ship and so on and so forth, opening and closing valves, etcetera, I missed a crucial valve out on my ship. I left it closed. The back pressure subsequently burst the hose at the manifold, thus sending IFO240, spraying all over my ship and the quayside. It even reached all the way to the bridge windows and covered them too, quickly turning to thick black tar in the morning's cold air. Fuck, I had just fucked it big time. Mr Cillit Bang himself couldn't clean up this mess in time.

Mayhem ensued. The ferry's departure was delayed, and now my cock was on the block. It was my fault. The crew member who had slept in wasn't to blame. He was a factor, yes, but it was my decision to go at it alone. The beating I gave him was not deserved. Kidding. Call it a life lesson, if you like. We learn from our fuck ups, that's why we have them. It's just human nature. Learn and continue forward, applying your lessons learned accordingly to enhance future decisions. It's that simple. Nobody was harmed, and the environmental damage was minimal. I will take that hit any day. I was reprimanded for gross misconduct and given a final warning. Now, Paddy lad. You have to be whiter than fucking white here, sunshine. Eyes were all on Paddy the Baddy once again.

So, this carried on good for a few months. Then something happened. Now, I am sorry to disappoint here, but I can't remember what that something was. My switchboard won't let me access it for some reason. It's nothing bad or weird like wanking off a donkey or anything like that. Whether it was a cheeky line of coke with a particular person or whatever, I just can't access that memory. Plus I don't want to push to access it either, as I believe I am being protected from it for some reason. Anyway, as you can probably guess by now, Paddy doesn't do things by halves. In no time at all, I was back firing on all drug cylinders. From zero to fucking turbo in a heartbeat. Nasty, cocky and unreliable as fuck. The company had enough, paid me severance and gave me my marching orders.

That afternoon, after being sacked once again, I met up with Anthony, the lad from my first stripe. The both of us ended up on a two-day bender. We were at the lap dancing clubs and every fucking where. Just on a mad one. On a totally different planet. Put it all to the back of your mind, Paddy. Just concentrate on that pair of fine-looking tits there right in front of your face.

After the bender, I then went back home to the parents. My mum was just galloping around the living room. She took one look at the state of me and basically just told me to fuck off and to get out of the house. So, I did. I went back to the pub to continue my bender. Then, for some bizarre reason, I decided that I wanted to go and test drive a car. Soooo, I headed to the Lexus dealership in Bootle, Liverpool. I showed my keen interest in a car on the forecourt. I must have looked like I had just been dug up. I was fucked and reeking of booze and extra-strong mints. The salesman didn't seem to care though. He just wanted to hit his target sales and get his commission.

So I convinced him to take me for a test drive. He slapped on the trade plates and off we went. I was driving. We drove to the city centre and back, a good twenty-minute round trip. I fucking like this car, I thought. I want it. So, I was giving it the old, 'Oh yar. Absolutely. Fantastic little engine in this here vehicle,' sort of shit.

We arrived back at the dealership, he jumped out and I drove off. Why did you do that, Paddy, you dickhead? Only fuck himself knows the answer to that one, people. I gave it the old *Grand Theft Auto* shite. In and out of traffic like a fucking lunatic. I got to Walton Hospital, about ten minutes away, bailed from the car and then walked over to Walton Park across the road. It was a lovely summer's afternoon. I remember just lying on the grass, off my fucking rocket, blowing smoke rings up at the police helicopter circling above that was obviously searching for this car. What a cocky bastard, eh?

Shortly afterwards, I returned to the pub to carry on with my bender for the rest of the day. Later that evening, I returned to the hospital. There was my Lexus, looking all beautiful in its showroom demonstrator condition. It still had the Lexus plates on the front and back. Private registration. Get rid of those fuckers. I ripped them off, climbed into the car and set off. The moon above was in its quarter form. Oh, neap tides, Paddy. That's not relevant any more, my mate.

I arrived at Kendell in the Lake District, parked up in a hotel car park and spent the night getting myself clued up on the Lexus operator systems, giving it that good old review.

The following morning, I went searching for donor plates. I had to get some fucking plates on this car; it looked dodgy as fuck. I was driving around the town of Kendell. Lovely little place. I wasn't here for the scenery though. I was here because, I think, looking back, I wanted to test drive this car on my own on the nice bendy roads of the Lake District. It may have had something to do with that game that I was playing in prison with the maths. I am not sure about this. But it just seems a bit logical to me now.

Anyway, I couldn't find a Lexus in Kendell. So I targeted a Saab that was sitting alone in a car park. The plates on the Saab were not screwed on like most plates on most models. They were simply glued on. So, they came off pretty easily from the Saab, and with a dab of superglue from a local shop they were glued back onto **MY** Lexus. Lovely job. A couple of hours of test driving around in the lakes first. I really like the way this Lexus looks and drives, Paddy, wouldn't you agree? Oh, absolutely, Paddo. It just rips with grip. The engine in this is absolutely fantastic. Blistering performance right of the line, Paddy. And the way it holds those gears in sports mode, whoosh, right up into the red rev range.

What an animal. Yes, totally, Paddo. It gives you feel, Paddo, feel, right through the steering wheel. Almost as though it's alive, it's part of you; the skin on your palms is almost synchronised with the leather on the wheel. More like the rubber on the road, Paddy, hahaha. Look, watch this. Into this hairpin bend at 65mph, the grip is just astounding, the body roll is near as damn it non-existent. It's almost as if the car is in flight somehow. Hahaha, yes, Paddy, a flying rocket, that's a good way to describe this. Hahahaha, I must say. It's very futuristic in its design too. These knobs and switches here are… Anyway. By the time my test drive was over I was in Scunthorpe. What? That's the other side of the country, Paddy. Yes, I know. Well, why Scunthorpe? Again, you will have to ask fuck for the answer to that one.

Scunthorpe is a bit like Blackpool but with more gobshites per population. I just cut about there for the day, feeding the pigeons and chatting to the local statues and shit. I had plenty of drugs on me. In fact, I think I had a different type of drug in each pocket, and I was wearing combat trousers and a coat. I checked into a hotel for the night.

'Just fill out this form please, sir, with your full address and your vehicle registration if you have it.'

'I got the train here, love, thanks.'

'Thank you, sir. Here is your key. You are in room??? Just down the corridor to the left. Would you like any breakfast in the morning, sir?'

'Erm. I actually prefer to have my breakfast before I go to bed. Just so that I can have a sleep in. Do you have any coconuts? Doesn't matter. Good night. Thank you.' I needed a fucking bath. My underpants were starting to look like my dad's, giving me unwanted feedback and growling. I climbed into the bath with the underpants on. Right, Paddy. Turn on the taps and let's fill this bad boy up.

Almost instantly, my knob started shouting up, 'Eh, Paddy, Paddy, Paddy. When are they taking the cover off the pool, mate eh?' Shhh, knob, it's not coming off in here, the pool's closed, mate. I will get a shower after this and you lot can play out in the rain for a bit, how's that? 'Ahrrrr. Ohh, all right then. Eh, Paddy. Did you see the titties on that girl in the lap dancing club the other night? Whorrr, I was standing up for hours just to get a better view.' Yes, I fucking know you were, you cheeky bastard.

The next day, after leaving the hotel room with the trouser press and the kettle in pieces, I headed off. All the local pigeons were out to see me off, giving me a flyby as I left the town. 'Lookadekoo, lookadekoo,' God speed, Paddy, God speed. I had to get home and ditch this fucking car. Give it a jet wash and fill the tank full of fuel, Paddy. Then Lexus will probably just forget about the whole thing.

I somehow ended up on this gravel type of road. I didn't have a fucking clue where I was. I had chosen to test drive the model without the sat nav fitted as standard. What a fool. This road went on and on for fucking miles, and then it just came to an end. No shit, the road just fucking ended. There was just a sort of farmer's gate and a huge field in front of me. Motherfucker, I have to go and head back all the way down this road again. I turned the car around and floored it.

Unfortunately, I overcooked it on a bend on the gravel and lost control. The car spun around and slid sideways down a ditch and into a fence. The windscreen smashed right by my face and then just cracked all the way across. Fuck me. I would need to edit my review. Fair fucking play to the Lexus four-wheel drivetrain though. The fucking car just drove right back out of this ditch and back on to the gravel road. I got out to inspect the damage. Windscreen fucked. Headlights smashed. Front number plate missing (sacrificial anyway, so bonus). Driver's wing mirror gone. Right-hand side all dented and scratched. The front of the car looked like it had taken a massive bite out of the grass and still had it hanging from its mouth. Fuck's sake, Paddy. After the jet wash we will need to apply copious amounts of T-Cut, I think.

I continued my drive home. I had to drive slowly because I could barely see the road ahead. Then it started to get dark. The headlights were not only smashed, but one was fucked altogether and the other was just sort of pointing directly at the floor. It was no good, this. I needed to pull over. So, I did. It was a Friday night. Not that I was keeping track of the days. I knew this because I always remember what the police officer said to me shortly afterwards. I pulled over in a layby on a B road, had a big fat couple of lines of vit C. I then put my seat back and, believe it or not, I fell straight asleep.

I awoke the next morning, still on the fucking moon. The sun was blazing through the cracked windscreen in a weird, trippy sort of way. Beams of light in different colours in front of me. Shit, my eyes are broken. I pressed the button to move my seat back into position. Lovely fucking action by the way, Lexus. Top marks for that one. I sat up and caught a glimpse of this police van coming in the opposite direction, the policeman in which then caught a glimpse of me.

We held eye contact for a bit too long as he passed, not in any sort of romantic, give us your phone number way. I am talking more of a, you look fucking dodgy, yes, I know, and so do you sort of look. That was close, I thought. I racked up a couple of lines for breakfast and opened a nice fresh bottle of orange juice (vitamins are essential). Next thing, I looked in the rear mirror and could see the front of the car. And there was this police van right behind me. Fucking story of my life, this.

Where was my cap gun? The officer came to my window, so I closed it and hung out my tongue as if I were asleep. You were only just looking at each other a few minutes ago, Paddy. Yes, I know. But like the prison officers, most police officers aren't really that bright. They copy off each other when they are doing their ascertaining exams and everything.

'Hello, hello, hello. And what do we have here?' he said as he squatted up and down. 'What's happened to this car? It's in a right state, isn't it?'

'Yep, it is, Officer. A crocodile ran right in front of this here vehicle just a few miles a back that way on Highway Six. I swerved to miss the son of a bitch but this here vehicle just toppled right on over. Gee whizz, I nearly shit ma pants, Officer, I truly did. Praise be to the Lord.'

He asked me to join him in the back of his vehicle. Why do they always ask you to do that and then they just get in the front? It doesn't make sense. 'Can you please tell me why you are driving a beaten-up brown Lexus (it wasn't like turd brown, people, it was more bronze) with the registration of a blue SAAB?'

'Erm. Erm, a mix up at the factory perhaps? No. Okay.' I was bang to rights and just fessed up. 'You don't get many results like this first thing on a Saturday morning, hahaha.' He laughed. Jolly good I could be of assistance, Officer. That's how I remember it was a Friday when I pulled over originally. Clever, eh?

A unit from Liverpool eventually came to collect me from whichever police station I was in. I haven't a fucking clue where this was. It was a male and a female officer. Both were sound to be fair. The lady officer even bought me a drink and a bar of chocolate from the garage. Unfortunately for me though, they were unwilling to let me drive. So, they banged me up in the cage at the rear of the van.

I remember the lady officer was chucking me peanuts through the cage. 'Careful there, don't get to close now. This one looks like a bit of a biter.' I spent the rest of that weekend in custody at S.A.S., or Saint Anne's Street Police Station. I had a microwave chilli con carne for my Sunday dinner. I know. Fucking outrageous, eh? The following day I was taken to Bootle Magistrates' Court. I was thinking, shit. This is it. Straight to jail. Do not pass go and do not collect one hundred pounds. I had well and truly completed my space mission and I was coming back down to earth on all thrusters. I was feeling properly fucked. I felt really, really bad if I am honest.

I was up in front of the magistrate a short while later. 'Mr Bennett. Rar, rar, rar de fucking rar. Now, seeing as it's your first offence, I am releasing you on bail with zero conditions until a court date for sentencing is made.' What the fuck did he just say to me, I thought. Paddy lad, he is serious. Just look at the floor and avoid all eye contact. Don't smile, for fuck's sake. Go back to that hospital bed, Paddy, with those three psychotic bitches, Paddy. Look sad.

So I walked straight out of that courtroom as a free man. For the time being anyway. Right, Paddy. Where did I park that shuttle? Earth is getting a bit too close now. I jumped into a cab and headed straight to a dealer's house. I then turned that space shuttle right around again a full 180° and engaged afterburners. Right back into space.

I overcooked the drugs quite a bit that evening. I was scatty, angry and just totally fucking manic. I was annoyed with everything and everyone. The tanker company for sacking me and everybody else. Cheeky bastards. How fucking dare they? So, with that I went to the docks. The security on the gates knew me. They didn't however know that I had been fired. So, with that, they just let me pass. 'Good evening, Paddy.'

The tanker company's office on the docks was made up of several Portakabins. These were separated into two different units. One was for the crews, changing rooms and canteen, etcetera, and the other was for the office staff and operations in general. It was closed at this time. No vessels were out operating either. So, I picked up a brick and chucked it through the office window, setting off all the alarms. I climbed through the window and grabbed the keys for the company van, plus a stapler. I don't know and don't ask. I just like staplers. They never let you down. I climbed into the van and off I went. Full tank of fuel too. How very thoughtful, and off I went, this time to Hull.

I don't particularly recall why I headed to Hull. I just did. I knew the place from previous visits on ship in the past. A lot of ignorant people say that the River Humber is the arsehole of the Earth and Hull is right up it. I don't agree with that. I don't really like Hull itself so much as a city. It's the people I like. I find them very friendly, honest and down-to-earth types. Hull is actually where my baby girl did her degree in biomedicine. She is now doing both her master's degree in Liverpool and also working as a junior doctor-type scientist in the Covid testing labs. Proud of you, my baby girl. You have come a long way from running over my toes in your baby walker and throwing up on my shoulders.

See, people. Now here is a prime example. My daughter had a fucked up father. Did she turn out stale? Nooo, did she, fuck. Stop using excuses. She does have an exceptional mother though to be fair, who is now with another guy, Garry. Now, Garry has been like a second father to my daughter over the years, looking out for her, picking her up from nights out on the town. Another fucking legend of a bloke in my eyes. Thank you so much, Garry.

So, back to Hull. I crossed the Humber suspension bridge. Fucking huge, this thing is. What a masterpiece in architecture. I paid the toll to cross. I am not a criminal. Anyway, I wasn't there long. I was driving like a bit of a divvy, not giving a fuck about anything. I turned into a one-way street heading in the wrong direction. There was a car coming my way. So, a question. If you see a car coming the other way down a one-way street, at speed, you fucking move over sharpish, don't you? Well, this guy didn't move fast enough, and I took the rear wing of his car off. I then slammed on my brakes, opened my window and called him a cunt. Then I continued to the Asda supermarket. I pulled up at the cash machine. Guess what for? Yep, cash. Just as I got my money, I was sideswiped by a rugby-playing police officer and introduced to the bracelets once again.

Soooo. That was me banged up again in custody in Hull. I was taken to Hull Magistrates' Court the following morning and remanded in custody for three weeks at HMP Hull. Another long one. HMP Hull. HMP Preston. HMP Lancaster and eventually HMP Liverpool.

The dealer of the Lexus who came on the test drive with me was named Gavin. I remember his name because I had to face the poor guy in court. I was partitioned behind the glass and he was there giving evidence against me. The poor guy was so nervous that he wouldn't even look my way. My solicitor, Brian Jackson, a very good, solid defence lawyer, tore poor Gavin to bits on cross-examination, effectively putting the blame on Gavin for stepping out from the vehicle first as opposed to the Lexus test drive policy of, the customer exits the vehicle first and then the salesman. This obviously had a very traumatic impact upon Gavin. I had caused that. I am so sorry, Gavin, I really am. Your face said it all. I hope you recovered from that sharpish, I really do.

CHAPTER 22
An easy sentence

I knew right from the very start that this sentence was going to be a long fucker. I knew I wasn't going to just walk out of the court like the rest. I also knew that I would have to return from the moon and face all those clouds once more. It was all my own doing, I know this. I wasn't and I am not looking for sympathy in any way. I just knew how much pain I was now going to have to face. So, I hatched a plan. That plan was to inform the custody sergeant of the bogus medical treatment I was receiving. The custody sergeant was then dutybound to call in a doctor for an assessment.

I offloaded to this GP with a load of lies, which he bought hook, line and sinker. 'So, Patrick. What medication are you receiving just now?'

Now, don't forget, you have the walking fucking Wikipedia of knowledge on all subjects relating to drugs here. 'I am currently prescribed 60mg of diazepam and 30mg of zopiclone per day, doctor.'

Now, just in case you are not aware of the effects of these drugs, I will tell you. Firstly, diazepam. It comes in both liquid and tablet form. The blue tablet is the strongest, 10mg. The yellow is 5mg and the white is 2mg. Everybody is born with a certain level of what's known as serotonin in their brain. It's a chemical. Let's call it your fight and your flight. Now, people that have high levels of serotonin naturally are those happy-go-lucky type of people. Those pricks who call their kids 'guys'. 'C'mon, guys, we're off rambling in the new forest.' Ned Flanders type of pricks. Friends of the earth. Fucking overkill with the recycling.

Then you have the other side, or the lower. They are the people that are born with low levels of serotonin, people who are depressed a lot, sad and down. I won't comment on this because it's a very real and sad condition, and I do really feel for those people. Then you have the normal, the sensible type of people who have average levels of serotonin, the ones who wash their cars on a Sunday and hoover the grass and bore, bore, bore. The pawns on the chessboard, if you will.

Now, the job of diazepam is to replace that serotonin in your brain by means of serotonin synthesis, tricking your brain that you have the required level. What it also does, which I didn't know, is over a period of time, it will deplete your own levels of serotonin to a degree. That's why you cannot, if taking them for a long, sustained period, you can fucking not just come off them. Your brain will be effectively broken until your natural levels of serotonin are replaced over time. That time depends on the individual. They are fucking dangerous and should not be messed with. They are so fucking dangerous, believe me.

The zopiclone tablets come in 7.5mg form. These are very strong sleeping tablets. Again, something that you should never ever, ever fucking play about with. If you sleep okay most of the time but a bit shitty on other days, then just leave it. Let your brain manage this by its own merits. Walking, jogging. Horlicks before bed. Anything but sleeping tablets. Because again, once your head and its gibbons are used to these, it is so hard for your brain to re-develop its natural sleeping process.

The doctor assessing me was, therefore, of the opinion that my bogus doctor was overprescribing me. Doctors, eh? I know, tut. Additionally, as I had also planned, as this was the weekend, he was unable to speak to my doctor to question this. So, with this being the case, the only option was to prescribe me medication. The dosage I was prescribed was 40mg of diazepam and 15mg of zopiclone. The dosage was divided at a rate of 20mg diazepam each and every morning and a further 20mg every evening with the two sleeping tablets.

I was put on a reduction programme through my sentence and finished on something like 12mg of diazepam in the mornings and 14mg of an evening with one sleeping tablet. My sentence was a fucking haze. I was like a zombie. I wouldn't have cared less if I were still there. Especially in HMP Liverpool, where I had an army of mates watching my back and looking after me. I had a good mate, Keith, inside. My good mate outside too. He was in for supplying class As and using extreme violence to rob other drug dealers of their ill-gotten gains and drugs.

The day I was released. This is one of the reasons why I fucking hate the prison service and the horrible, scummy cunts who run it. If I saw those bastards floating out here at sea, I would use my skills in the knowledge and application of propulsion and thrust and chop the fucking cunts to pieces. Fish food. Fucking low-level rat fucking bottom feeders, the lot of them.

The procedure when you are released from jail is as follows. Around six a.m., all the prisoners in the prison who are due to be released that day, plus the prisoners taken to attend court, are collected from their cells respectively and taken to one big reception area, all apart from the sex-offending fucking breads that are protected and taken somewhere separately for their own protection. Sick fucks.

Anyway, one by one, each prisoner is taken to be processed for release and/or court. Once processed, the prisoner is then locked into another big waiting room until everybody from the start has been processed. You are all then locked in this second room. Then again, one by one, you are taken to receive the property that you came into prison with. Then you are interviewed by the P.O., or the principal officer. The head of the cunts. After this, you are locked back away in that second room until all prisoners are done.

When you receive your property, you are supposed to receive a week's worth of the prescribed drugs that you have been taking, together with a letter for your doctor. The idea of the latter is to give every prisoner that is on medication the chance to arrange an appointment with their GP, hence the week's supply. I was subsequently processed with no medication. Where're my meds? They will be given to you shortly. So, now the time comes that all prisoners have been processed. It's time to walk the slow walk from the reception and on to that big gate to freedom.

Where're my meds? You will have to wait a few hours because the medical staff are in a meeting. Are you taking the fucking piss? I want to go. I have done my sentence. Well, fucking go then, I was told. I don't care, you are all the same to me. Now, I won't mention this cunt's name, but if I ever, and I mean ever, see this twat around the streets, consequence analysis will be superseded and he is fucking getting it. Yes, I did say that. You cunt. Is it any wonder prisons are fucked? Again, pay peanuts you get fucking monkeys. Monkeys could operate it better than these horrible braindead bastards though. Fucking parasites. The cockroaches in the walls hold more respect than those cunts. Grrrr. I fucking hate them.

I had nowhere to go upon my release. No house. No car. No family, through my own doing, and Emma wouldn't let me see Amy unless it was controlled through a contact centre. Not because she was being a bitch, but because it was the sensible thing to do. I hadn't seen my baby girl for a long time, plus Emma didn't know my state of mind at that time. I was homed in the YMCA, a robbing bastard charity hostel in Liverpool city centre. Charity should not be in the title, because like most of these charities, it is just about profit and greed. Very little filters through to the actual needy.

The next morning, after waking up in this hostel, I didn't feel good. I just couldn't be bothered with anything. I am going to keep this part short, people, because I can feel myself becoming emotional here. My switchboard is trying to slam the brakes on here; I will try my best. Basically, after a couple of weeks, I had barely moved from the bed. I was in a place I can never describe. I was just lying there, looking out of the window, listening to people laughing and shouting outside in the city centre.

It was summer. I would fucking pray for the dark. God grant me the serenity for the things I cannot change, give me courage to change the things that I can and the wisdom to know the difference. I would just lay there, whispering over and over again. I was fucked. But I didn't understand why. The diazepam had depleted my serotonin. I had very little. I didn't know this; I just thought I had finally broken myself. I didn't want this any more. I couldn't.

I walked from the hostel to my parents' house in the pissing-down rain, just a t-shirt, shorts and flip flops on, the same that I had been wearing since arriving at the hostel. It was early hours. I was soaked wet through. I didn't care; it would all be over soon.

Now, this wasn't a fucking cry for help. This was the real deal. That's why I can empathise so much with people who have this constantly. They fucking need that help, they really do. Even if they don't want to talk, you just can't let them down. I climbed over the back wall at my parents' house. I just stood there for God knows how long, looking up at that window, where it all began. The planes flying overhead. Our holiday to Spain. The memories. I didn't want to hurt anyone by what I was about to do; my head told me to go there. It just made sense at that time. It was the only thing that did. Just end it where it all began.

There was a bench under the kitchen window. I just remember laying on it, sobbing, a bit too loudly, just hoping somebody would hear me, come out and put an arm around me. Come on, son, let's get you inside. We can fix this. But it never happened. I must have been on that bench for a good couple of hours. Something was just putting me off doing it. I think deep down it was my baby girl. That school uniform. 'Dadth, wook at my picthure.' I needed to turn this around. It was now or never.

So, I stood on that bench, gripped the kitchen window and pulled it open. I then climbed through and went into the kitchen cupboard, where I knew my dad kept his taxi earnings. I took every penny. This time, it was the drug that was going to save my life.

Within the hour, the drugs had levelled me out, more or less, those dark, fucked up thoughts just easing off slowly. I suppose in a way the drugs had just given me back life after taking so much of mine away from me over the years. The realisation of what I had just done to my parents didn't hit me. It couldn't. I was bulletproof from such emotion whilst back in space. Like fucking Batfink. Wings of steel.

I met up with my mate, Keith, a couple of days later. He had his own house and lived alone, so I basically moved in with him. It was just a constant party at his house, people just coming and going at all hours, day and night. One night, at one of his parties, I met a girl called Anne, a beautiful girl in both body and mind. And what a fucking cracking arse she had. Anyway, we got together. She was a stewardess and away a lot, but when she was home it was great. I ended up staying at her's most of the time too when she was home. Things were looking up again.

After a few months, my head, although still in space a bit, was levelling out. Anne was good for me. She helped me to research and understand what had happened to me with the diazepam. Shocking stuff. Again, please just stay the fuck away from those things unless you're aware of what they do. You won't find this information on the advice note that comes with the tablets.

Emma was letting me see Amy properly after the contact centre. I needed to start contributing towards her again and get myself independent and into my own house. So, I made a few phone calls and within a couple of days I had a boat. This boat was back out in the North Sea. It was the same rotations as before, one month on, one month off. The company booked me a flight from Liverpool up to Aberdeen. That's when Ryanair was trading on that route. I was starting over again. I felt good about this, a fresh start.

I arrived at the airport in Liverpool. I didn't have my passport, as this had disappeared somewhere in the turmoil of my life. I did however have all my seaman's paperwork and my licences. I had travelled all over Europe on these alone in the past, which is legal to do as long as you are travelling to or from a vessel. Anyway, I was checking in. The guy (a gay, gay guy), I am saying gay guy because of the following. This guy wasn't gay. He was gay, gay. Effeminate gay. Now, I am not homophobic by any means. I have good friends and close family who are gay. However, the gay, gay, fucking feminine mincy types, well, I just can't handle them at the best of times. Acting all fruity and making vulgar remarks because they are in this middle fucking can't make up what they are type of thing and think they can just mince about being all flamboyant and rude.

So anyway, this gay, gay check-in assistant was having issues checking me in due to the documents. Fair enough. 'I will have to call my supervisor.' Again, fair enough. His supervisor arrived, who was another fucking gay, gay. Fuck's sake. Fair enough. Then the two of them started sniggering and touching each other in that gay, gay sort of way. Now, don't forget, there is queue of people behind me here waiting to check in.

These two fucking clowns hadn't even acknowledged that fact; they were too concerned with mincing around with my documents as if it was an episode of *Glee*. Then, the supervisor, the gayest out of the two gay, gays, looks at my seaman's discharge book.

Now, this book I have had all my life. I am actually on my second one now to be fair. Anyway, it's a book that records each and every vessel that you have served on and is an official document. Its title, *Seaman's Discharge Book*, is what it is. When you are discharged from a vessel, your seaman's book is stamped and recorded. No one has ever questioned the title in my life, no one. This gay, gay fucking dirty-minded, vulgar bastard sees the title and is laughing at the title. Seaman as in semen, ejaculatory shit. I don't have to explain that, surely? And discharge as, well, you guess. The both of them were sniggering like a pair of kids over this. The hairs on my neck stood to attention. I growled at the two of them and called them a pair of cunts and was asked to leave the airport because I was being aggressive and abusive. This pair of cunts had just offended me.

Anyway. Shit, what was I going to do? I phoned Emma. 'Paddy, just calm down. Get yourself to the train station and there will be a ticket to Aberdeen waiting for you.' So, I did, and there was. She also sorted me out an apartment, so that a couple of weeks later I had a place to come back to where Amy could stay over. Thanks, Emma.

This was good for a year or so until I had another trauma at sea. I was going to share this with you. Give you the details of how it happened and my thoughts about it. However, after the last chapter, I think my brain has had enough of this for the time being. There is no need for me to open this dialogue up. Basically, a great guy, a great seaman and a friend of mine, Mike Tarrager, was crushed to death inches away from me. It was my fault in a big way, as I was in charge of the operation and had told him to stand where he was standing just moments before. I am so sorry, Mike, I just never saw it coming. R.I.P., my mate.

Anyway, after this, I did what Paddy does to deal with such traumas. I booked myself on a six-month all-inclusive trip to the moon. Anne was good for me at this point. She was helping me in a big way to see straight. She was never into drugs. She had the occasional line of coke but that was it. Very sensible. Her switchboard was solid, should we say. I had plenty of money from working away so I was just getting fucked up on all kinds of drink and drugs. During this space flight, Anne was starting to pull away, if you like. She was getting pissed off and upset with my drug taking and my instability as a person. I can't blame her for that. I was just being a total gobshite to be fair.

I had been on a fucking crazy trip for a few days. No sleep whatsoever. Now, when you don't sleep for that long, and I am talking zero sleep, not even a fucking yawn, your brain, as I have mentioned earlier, starts to shut down. Your body is still, however, active. A certain part of your brain though, fails to inform the other part. You then start to hallucinate and hear stuff. Mad crazy shit.

So, here is Anne, away at work for a few days. She lived in this three-storey Victorian house in Crosby, Liverpool. This house was divided into three separate apartments. She lived on the middle floor. The co-habiting man and woman who lived above Anne in this house were youngish but old before their time, if you like, basically, a pair of moaning miserable bastards. I had, many a time before, called this lad a cunt, just because he complained so much.

Now, I felt a bit guilty about the way Anne was feeling. I had upset her. Other people, I imagine, in this case would do something nice such as book a meal in a nice restaurant for the two of you. Flowers and chocolates and a bottle of Bolly. A sorry card perhaps. Not balloons and teddy bears though. That's a bit too farfetched. A new twin tub washing machine maybe, have her hoover serviced for her, you know, all that romantic stuff. But not me. Nooooo... Paddy has to think outside of the box. I know. I will break into her flat whilst she is at work and decorate it for her.

Access to Anne's flat was by a steel set of exterior stairs, like a fire escape sort of set up. I would often walk behind her when coming up these stairs, just watching that fine booty do its thing, plus to catch her if she fell backwards, of course. So, I pulled up outside. I got my toolbox, paint and shit from the boot and carried them to the top of this fire escape. I needed access now to get through the communal door shared by Anne and the cunts upstairs. Once through this door, I would then just shoulder-barge Anne's door and fix the lock later.

I was banging the shit out of this communal door to try and attract the attention of the cunts above so that they would come and open it for me. There was frosted glass at the top of this door. Now, I was hallucinating just then. The problem was, as mentioned, the other part of my brain that had shut down hadn't informed the other part. Therefore, I didn't know. Now, through the pixelated glass, it looked as if, to me, the cunts behind from upstairs were looking at me through this glass and laughing at me. So I started to get a bit nasty and started to boot the door, calling it all sorts of cunts.

Obviously, there was no one behind it laughing at me. A few seconds later, after me giving the door a stern warning, it opened. The female from upstairs was behind it. 'Where's your fucking man, the fucking cunt?'

'He is in work.' The poor girl looked shocked.

'You fucking liar. Out of the way, cunt.' I just barged past her and BANG, right into Anne's flat. Tools and paint down on the floor, Paddy. Now, do your thing, Paddy, room for room.

Well, the geography in this room is all wrong. Would you agree, Paddy? Tut, tut, tut, oh yar, Padster, absolutely. It is sooooo 1994. Just a mismatch of awful colours, Padster. Oh yes. I do agree with you there, ohhhh and that light; those beautiful sash windows are just being exploited by those nasty curtains, don't you think? Ohhh my dearie me. Art nouveau? More like art no, no, hahahaha. Padster, you are soooo right. This is just one big noooo, noooo.

Right, next room. Oh, Padster, I just can't look. It's dreadful. My eyeballs are just sooo offended. They are almost teary. Vulgar, just vulgar, one would say. It's like something from a 1970s porn movie. Set the scene, Padster. Guy comes in to the room wearing dungarees, a straw hanging loosely from his lips, shirtless and muscular, a large spanner in his hand. Huge moustache. German. I havezz comezzz to fiverd zee fridgez...

Right, get to work, Paddy. I fucking totalled the place in an hour. Sixty-minute fuck up. I fucking destroyed it. I found a set of drumsticks, wooden. They may have even been just big chopsticks; fucked if I know. Anyway, they can be screwed on to the wall with the lid of a tea pot next to them. Now, that's art. She will love this. A dash of blue paint here, lime green there. Totally transformed, Paddy. Fuck me, looking back, it looked like fucking *Rainbow* meets *Tweenies*.

Anyway, during the revamp I heard a noise. There was a car outside. I could hear talking. I stopped. No noise other than paint dripping off my brush onto the carpet. Don't worry about that, Paddy. A bit of T-Cut will sort that out. Then I heard the talking again. Hang on, they were talking about me here. Then I heard, or thought I had heard, someone saying, let's go and get him, he is upstairs. Oh fuck. They were coming up here.

So, I dived into the bedroom. Fuck, Anne, what you have got yourself involved in here? Thanks for giving me the fucking heads up. So, I am in this bedroom, psyching myself up ready for battle, paintbrush in hand, held above my head like a weapon. What are you going to do with this, Paddy? Fucking paint them? Then these two figures appeared in the door frame. I can't recall the faces because they were not real. Anyway, one of them had a rubber gun. He was pointing this gun at me, and it's flexing and bouncing at the end like an elastic band. However, I am like, 'C'mon, lads. Take it easy. Don't shoot; we can work the problem here.'

Then they just disappeared, a bit like Peter the oddball. So, I walked out of that room and looked into the next room. In there was a woman sitting on the floor. Next to her was a child with a bin bag on its head. Fuck fucking me. These were just weird bastards. I ran out of the flat and down the fire escape and over to my car. Shit, the keys were in the flat with my fucking phone.

Next thing, the cunt with the rubber gun popped his head over the bush in the front garden and pointed the shooter at me. So I ducked behind my car. There were also kids playing in the street here. Or maybe they were just planted there; I didn't know. I didn't want them caught up in the crossfire. 'Fucking move, kids, run, back in your house.' Then I shouted at the bush, 'C'mon then, dickhead, drop the fucking shooter and let's just have it, you and me.' The neighbours must have been looking out from their windows thinking, what the fuck?

You are going to get fucking clipped here, Paddy, he isn't scared of your paintbrush. Fucking run. So I broke cover, fucking bolting up the street, running zig-zag formation so I didn't get shot. There was a phone box around the corner. I phoned Keith. 'Keith, mate, there is a load of crackheads just bailed into Anne's flat with rubber guns. Get down here now, lad, with some tools and we will rub the fuckers out.'

'Paddy. You are fucking on one, mate. You have been for days. Just get yourself home and go to bed.'

'Keith, you fucking cunt.' I needed my car keys. Too fucking dangerous to go back to that flat though. So, what did I do? I went to the police.

I ran into the local police station, all out of breath and erratic. 'There are fucking crackheads, armed fucking crack-heads, in my bird's flat.' They sanctioned a full armed response team, which blue-lighted it the short distance to the property. I followed a short while later in the back of another police car. As we pulled up outside Anne's, there was an army of armed police heading back down the fire escape from the annexe flat.

One of the officers get me out from the back of the car. 'There is no one up there, son. It's just a mess up there with paint and a broken lock.' Then I spotted one of them climbing out of a side window.

'Look, there's one of the cunts climbing out of the window there'.

'There isn't a window there, son,' he said. Next thing. 'Right, Patrick. You have two options here. Option one is you are getting nicked. Option two is you will let us take you to a hospital, as you are obviously not right.'

'Well, it's option fucking two then, isn't it, Officer?' They took me to Aintree Hospital to be checked over by the doctors. 'Can I have a look at your gun please, mate?'

'Piss off.'

I was in the hospital for a couple of hours. I didn't see anything weird in the hospital apart from a sheep kicking the fuck out of a turkey in the toilets. 'Oi, leave him alone, you fucking woolly bully.' I was given the all clear and discharged. I then went to Keith's and slept for three days solid. When I awoke, there was a note from Anne. Paddy. I loved the flat, really creative, However, it breaks my heart, but I have to leave you. You are just fucking mental.

And that, people, is it for now. After this, I went back to sea, only this time I travelled all over the world and still do today. I did want to share my times whilst working with the Royal Marines and the Kenyan Navy of Somalia, shooting at a Chinese fishing boat off the coast of Somalia, thinking it was a pirate ship. Being accused of trying to blow up a plane on a flight from Dubai to Mombasa. My travels around Malaysia, Singapore, where I was chased around a hotel room by a girl with a dick. The Persian Gulf, Sri Lanka, India. Unfortunately, I don't have the space. If my baby girl will allow me to write another book, then I will. If she doesn't want me to, then I won't. It's that simple. Although I will write one just for you, baby girl. Your own unique copy. I love you so much. Dad. XXXX

THE END